PARENTING YOUR
POWERFUL
CHILD

PARENTING YOUR
POWERFUL
CHILD

Bringing an End to the Everyday Battles

Dr. Kevin Leman

Revell

a division of Baker Publishing Group
Grand Rapids, Michigan

© 2013 by Dr. Kevin Leman

Published by Revell
a division of Baker Publishing Group
P.O. Box 6287, Grand Rapids, MI 49516-6287
www.revellbooks.com

Printed in the United States of America

Library of Congress Cataloging-in-Publication Data is on file at the Library of Congress, Washington, DC.

ISBN 978-0-8007-2020-9 (cloth)
ISBN 978-0-8007-2316-3 (pbk.)

To protect the privacy of those who have shared their stories with the author, some details and names have been changed.

13 14 15 16 17 18 19   7 6 5 4 3 2 1

To the entire Leman family—
each of you a powerful force for the
good in your own unique way

Contents

Acknowledgments

To my editor, Ramona Cramer Tucker, a discerning mom to multi-talented Kayla and a relentless powerhouse determined to make a difference in the world.

To my Revell editor, Lonnie Hull DuPont, who believes in this author and encourages my individual bent, even when it's more "bent" than she bargained for.

To my project editor, Jessica English, whose new last name matches her precise skills.

Introduction

Is Your Kid Powering Up?

It's time to take the buzzard by the beak.

Every family has a powerful kid.

He's the one who flings himself in the door, demands the car keys, and then argues with you that his trip to his buddy's to practice basketball is more important than your trip to the grocery store.

She's the one who, at 2 years old, stomped her foot and said, "Do it by self."

He's the one who drags his feet and can't find things as you're trying to get him out the door to school so you can go to work.

She's the one the principal calls about, because she's been caught writing unacceptable emails.

He's the one who says he'll take out the trash but never manages to do it.

She's the one who disses you at Target, then expects you to buy her the hottest new shirt.

He's the one who talks back, no matter what you say.

She's the one you sigh over at night.

He's the one you worry about when it's 1:00 a.m. and he still hasn't checked in.

She's the one who's so sensitive that the entire family walks on eggshells around her.

He's the one who's even more stubborn than you are.

Do any of these sound familiar?

If so, you of all people can understand that there's a reason some animal mothers eat their young.

Power can come from a lot of places and can look different in the ways it plays out, but the effect on the child, you, and your entire family is the same. Here's what I mean.

> **There's a reason some animal mothers eat their young.**

When my kids were little—I have five of them, spread across a wide age gap—I loved making even the shortest car trips fun. It helped that my kids were young enough to be gullible. For example, when we'd drive up to a red light, I'd lean over and give a little *puff*, and the light would magically change to green. The kids were amazed at the power of their dad. Of course, they didn't know that I'd been watching the light from the perpendicular direction change to yellow, so I knew ours would become green at that very instant.

On those car trips, we'd frequently pass by a power plant in Tucson, Arizona. The first time, the kids asked, "Oh, Dad, what's that?"

"The hamburger factory," I quipped.

"Ooohhh," they said in unison awe.

They called it that for a long time.

You see how much power parents have?

But so did that power plant. It wasn't very big, but wow, look at all the houses, businesses, and streetlights that were powered by that seemingly small unit!

It's the same with your powerful child. He—no matter what age or stage—is powerfully affecting much more than you think. He's the child who is orchestrating your entire household by his antics—or the fear of his antics. She's the one who so frustrates you that you take it out on other family members because you don't want to face a blowout with her. It's simply too exhausting. So that powerful 2-year-old, 5-year-old, 8-year-old, 11-year-old, 15-year-old, or 19-year-old is controlling all your family as a result.

That's why *now* is the time to take your buzzard by the beak—to take those power surges and transform them into positive urges. After all, power plays only continue when they're working.

But what if that innate power could be redirected to develop your child's natural talents? To help him stand firm against peer pressure in the most crucial years? To give back to the family not grudgingly but with a smile? To make a difference in your community? Think

> **Power plays only continue when they're working.**

of all that power causing you grief and frustration being harnessed for the good. You'll be amazed at what your child can accomplish!

Someday you're going to spend a lot of time picking out the dress or tux you'll wear to that child's wedding. I know you'll look wonderful in it. But better than that, you're going to say to yourself with great satisfaction, "I did my job well as a parent, didn't I?"

That's because you, parent, are smart. You did the things you had to do, even when you were frustrated, angry, and annoyed, your back was against the wall, and the chips were down. You hung in there. That's because you were convinced that your child was worth the effort, no matter what others felt or said to the contrary.

You never know who could be in your home right now. The very child demanding a drink of water and a bedtime story as you try to read this book could be the next president of the United States, set to manage multiple tasks. The one you have to coax to interact with others and who prefers to stay in his room might be the next Bill Gates, set to change computer technology as we know it. The one who argues with you nonstop might someday be a state attorney. The kid who thought he could fly off your roof—even though you warned him that all that goes up must come down—might be the next Albert Einstein. The sassy child who is always challenging the system might be the next Rosa Parks. The kid who mixed chemicals in your garage—even when you told him not to—and blew out the garage door might be the one who discovers an entirely new form of environment-friendly fuel. And the child who is always spelunking in mud, sticking poison oak sprigs in his pocket (you know because you got the blistery rash when you did his laundry), and leaving streaks of manure from the neighbor's garden he blew through on the way to your kitchen might be the one who discovers the cure to cancer.

Think of all the energy you have harnessed in your very own power plant—and what it might mean someday.

Parenting Your Powerful Child reveals:

- who your powerful child is (it may not be the one you think).
- why she does what she does.
- what genes and environment have to do with it.
- his own personal screenplay on life (a key to resolving those behaviors that drive you nuts).
- her goals behind the scenes.

It'll help you:

- understand your powerful child like you never have before.
- talk to your child in a language that works for both of you.
- redirect his power surges into something that positively impacts all around him.
- meet her needs for belonging and unconditional acceptance.
- give you the long view you need as a parent in the trenches.

I guarantee it.

1

The Anatomy of a Powerful Child

Powerful kids don't just happen;
they're created.

Imagine you are sitting at a baseball game. The batter goes berserk when he strikes out for the third time. After smacking the ground with his bat a couple times, he slings it—and hits one of his own teammates in the dugout.

What's the reaction of the crowd? Stunned silence.

There's an old ad for the stock brokerage firm E. F. Hutton & Co. that claims, "When E. F. Hutton talks, everyone listens." That's the way it is with powerful people. When they talk, people listen.

Let's say you were having a conversation, and all of a sudden the person you're talking to starts screaming. How would you react? You'd probably drop your jaw in shock if you were unused to such behavior from that person. But if it was the norm, you might respond differently.

You might take it, fight back, or sigh and hope that person will get the barrage of words and attitude over with quickly and then go away.

An adult who throws a temper tantrum at home or work, a teenager who has to have things his way all the time, an 8-year-old who throws a baseball bat, a 3-year-old who refuses to go potty—all these are examples of powerful people. There are a lot of ways to be powerful. Some are easy to spot because they are overly demonstrative, such as the berserk batter. But those who use subtle control are just as manipulative and powerful.

It Starts in the High Chair

Take, for instance, the 17-month-old boy who refuses to eat, whether it's Beech-Nut baby food or home-pureed broccoli. So what do we parents do? We get creative.

"Open up the hangar, because the plane is about to land!" We make fools of ourselves, circling the food around like a jet plane and trying to zoom it into the kid's open mouth.

What happens? The kid isn't stupid. He opens his mouth to play the game. But as soon as that spoon gets close, what does he do? He shuts his mouth, and the food splatters all over the high chair tray. You can even see it in his eyes: *You're not going to get me to eat that stuff. Never. Nuh-uh.*

So the well-meaning parent actually creates power struggles with that child from an early age.

You lift up your 15-month-old daughter's bottom to put Pampers on her, realize you're missing that wonderful-smelling baby powder, and tell her to stay put. You come back into the room a minute later, and where is she? MIA. You find her hiding behind the couch, capture her, and carry her back to the diaper-changing station in her bedroom.

You spend the next five exasperating minutes wrestling her as she squirms, trying to get the tabs aligned on the diaper so they'll hold.

What is your daughter saying? "You're not going to tell me what to do. I'm my own person."

At a very early age, children can start to have perfectionistic tendencies. They have to sit in the same chair at the dinner table. Their stuffed animals have to be lined up just so, or they can't sleep. You have to make macaroni and cheese exactly the same way every time, since any deviation can upset their world.

> **At a very early age, children can start to have perfectionistic tendencies.**

Consider this scenario. Twenty-one-month-old Buford is sitting in his high chair, ready for lunch.

"There you go," you say and deliver his sandwich on his favorite Clifford the Red Dog melamine plate, complete with a matching bowl of Goldfish crackers.

Then as you step one foot away, ready to prepare your own lunch—because of course you think of your child first—the meltdown begins. He starts crying and then screams. He bangs his head on the tray of the high chair and the food scatters across your linoleum floor. What on earth?

After picking up the food from the floor, you put it back on his favorite plate and hand it to him again with a smile. *Maybe he's just tired and needs a nap*, you think. But he hasn't shown any signs of being tired before now.

He takes one look, narrows his eyes, shoves the food onto the floor for round two, and starts screaming again.

Then it hits you. Usually you cut the crusts off his bread and cut his sandwich into four little triangles. Today you were in a rush, so you forgot.

You whisk the sandwich off the floor, since in your house you believe in the two-second rule. If it's only been on the floor for two seconds each time, it's still edible. Whipping out a knife, you cut off the crusts, trim the sandwich into neat little triangles, and position it per usual on his plate.

This time when you bring it to little Buford, the kid is smiling ear to ear. He has triangles. Life is good.

What happened here? By always trimming the kid's sandwich into perfect shapes, you're saying, "You can have life exactly like you want it."

But is every one of your days predictable? Does life give you exactly what you want when you want it? Then why would you paint that picture for your child?

She's Got Your Number

Consider another scenario.

Your 6-year-old insists she has to have a certain toy. All the other kids in her kindergarten have one.

"No, I'm not going to buy you that," you say.

Twenty minutes later, not only has she continually barraged you with her request, but you've discovered that the meal you were trying to throw together to make your hungry hubby happy is missing a key ingredient—his favorite barbecue sauce. You were at the grocery store yesterday and bought an alternate brand, but you know how picky he can be. So you load the kid up in the car and drive to the Super Target to get the special sauce.

What happens along the way in the cart?

You wear down.

"Okay," you finally agree, "we'll go to the toy aisle and look."

Three minutes later, the toy is in the cart with your happy daughter hugging it.

"That's the last toy I'm buying you for life," you say as you head to the checkout aisle.

Notice what has happened.

Twenty minutes earlier, you told the kid, "I'm not buying you anything."

Now, if you look at the receipt, you see a line item: "Toy . . . $19.99."

You actually bought the stupid thing that you know she'll be tired of within a week.

So what have you taught your powerful child? If she reads you right, she'll know when you're at your lowest emotionally. That's the best time to hit you again and keep hitting you. If she works hard, she has a good chance of pulling off what she wants.

What's your child thinking? *Hey, this works. If I keep asking and don't give up, I'll get what I want.*

That's how a powerful kid works. She uses everyday life instances to work you in such a way that you give in—because sometimes giving in is easier.

Parents tell me all the time, "I know I shouldn't do it, but sometimes I get so tired, I give in. It's the constant pestering that wears me down. All I can think is, *Please shut up.*"

Powerful kids have your number; don't think they don't. Yes, it's easier in the short run to give in. It shuts them up temporarily (until they

> **What's your child thinking?**
> *Hey, this works. If I keep asking and don't give up, I'll get what I want.*

want the next thing). But neither of you win with that strategy. You might gain a breather for an hour or two before the demands begin again, but you set yourself up for the next situation. You've given your child more power—a deep-seated attitude that she has to win and additional confidence that she will win if she follows her plan.

In the long run, it would be better to put your pestering child in a room and let her howl at the moon all night when she doesn't get what she wants. The next morning, when she asks again for that toy, looking oh-so-pitiful with those red-rimmed eyes, you do the smart thing. You say, "No, I'm not getting you that toy," and you walk away to make breakfast for the entire family.

See how it works?

So take a look at your own powerful child. What five or six specific instances can you see from the recent past where, through powerful behavior, that child received what she wanted because you got worn down and gave in?

How did that influence your child's powerful techniques? Did it lessen them or ramp them up?

Ah, now you're getting it.

It Will Only Ramp Up from Here

All lessons in life aren't learned easily, and this is one that's better for your child to learn early: "You don't get what you want when you want it. The world doesn't revolve around you."

Kids who don't learn that grow to be powerful elementary school kids.

Like Samuel, who lorded it over everybody in his third-grade class until finally another powerful child got sick of it and said, "No! I'm not gonna do that. You're not the boss of me. You're so stuck-up. Nobody else likes you either." The boy's world crumbled in that instant, because he'd never been told no, and he expected everybody to do what he wanted when he wanted it. And why wouldn't he? His parents and older sister had babied him and given him everything he wanted. He was in charge at home.

Kids who are powerful elementary school kids grow into even more powerful junior highers.

The junior high world can be a terribly cruel one, where boys compete in the physical realm to be number one and girls compete in the emotional realm to be part of the popular cliques. When I was in private practice, many of my clients were parents and their adolescent children, since those critical years can be tumultuous for both parent and child.

Gabriela, for example, had always sought attention. By eighth grade, she had climbed to the top of the food chain in her particular group. She was known for getting attention in all the wrong ways but somehow got away with it . . . until she pulled one power play too many. When she texted inappropriate comments that made fun of a girl outside her group and publicly shamed the girl at school, she got more than she bargained for. A week later, Gabriela's mom got a shocking call from an attorney, who informed her the girl's family was pressing harassment charges against Gabriela.

"At first I didn't believe it," Gabriela's mom tearfully said. "I knew my girl could never text messages like that. But then I saw them, and my eyes were opened to who my daughter had become."

Kids who are powerful junior highers grow into even more powerful high schoolers.

Janet was powerful and an attention-getter. She had to be the first of her group of friends to try anything. One night at her father's remote cabin, she and her friends had a party that combined alcohol and synthetic drugs. Janet got dizzy and fell off her parents' high deck to the mountain path below. When she woke up in the hospital, she couldn't even remember how she'd been injured.

Sometimes, as I discovered in my private practice, the quiet children could be the most controlling. For example, at 8 years old, Shane was a quiet kid. But I could tell that he—not his parents—was clearly in charge of his home. His silence ran deep and lay heavy on the entire family. When Shane grew silent and retreated to his room, his mom constantly brought him things to try to make him happy. No matter what I said, she couldn't see that she was being manipulated. So year after year, she made it her goal to make her shy, "sensitive" son happy.

He paid her back for her efforts the day after he graduated from high school by leaving her a short note: *To Mom, who tried—and failed. I'm outta here.*

The emotional impact that note had on his mother was devastating, to say the least. Without intervention from God Almighty, she'll never recover.

I've shared the above two examples not to scare you but to emphasize the importance of making changes in your family dynamics *now*. Don't wait. Too much is at stake.

Powerful young kids become powerful junior highers, who become powerful high schoolers, who become powerful adults. Each time the ante of power is upped, the consequences of that power become more potentially life-changing.

A power-driven child who is 16 to 18 years of age is even more at risk, because he or she is driven to be in control and stay in control of life situations.

A teenage girl who feels powerless—as if her life is mapped out for her and she has no say over it—sometimes becomes anorexic or bulimic. She may also become a cutter—inflicting cuts with razor blades on places on her body that are easy to hide with clothing, such as her stomach, arms, or legs. Anorexia, bulimia, and cutting help her feel in control of something when situations in her home or relationships with her family or peers are out of her control. But such behaviors are emotionally and physically devastating.

> **Powerful young kids become powerful junior highers, who become powerful high schoolers, who become powerful adults.**

With a powerful teenage boy, the drive for power can lead to being reckless with the car. He might try to show how fearless and brave he is by passing a car on a hill, not knowing what's coming over the other side. In reality, he's only being stupid. He might also create bravado by duking it out with somebody instead of finding a way to avoid a fight or confrontation.

Ask any boy or young man if he's ever been in a fistfight, and that gleam will appear in his eye. Most young men get into a fight at some time, because in the male world, boys continually compete for dominance. However, times have changed since my high school days, when somebody dared a guy to knock my lights out—and he did. Today's kids are armed with knives and guns, and you wouldn't want your child on either end of one of those. Curbing powerful, attention-getting behavior is critical at every stage.

If It Walks Like a Duck . . .

Let me state for the record that adolescents have been weird for centuries. They'll continue to be weird. They'll roll eyes, slam doors, and talk in "never" and "always" extremes. All kids are prone to fling the "You never let me do anything" comment out at least a time or two . . . per day.

Parents who take those types of statements further to prove a point and "win" will never win. If they try, all they'll succeed in doing is ramping up their kid's power by teaching the kid how to become powerful. How to throw cheap shots.

Adolescents have been weird for centuries.

"You ungrateful little snot! I sent you to a camp that costs $750 for a week. How dare you say that!"

It's a shot below the belt that may feel good to you momentarily (hey, we're all human), but it changes how you interact with your child.

Instead of reacting to what your hormone-group child does, understand that she gets weird. When she hits pubescence and adolescence, hormones race around in her body. Since she doesn't know what to do with those strange, new urges, she hits the people closest to her.

So the next time your powerful kid rolls her eyes, don't take it personally. Say instead, "Oh, gosh, that was good. Do it again—only in slow motion this time. And if you could do it with hand gestures, I'd appreciate it even more."

Chill out. Take things in stride. Know what and who you're dealing with.

If it walks like a duck and quacks like a duck, I've got news for you. It is a duck.

Not a raccoon.

Even though your teenager may act more like a raccoon at the moment.

Slow Leak or Blowout?

I've had slow leaks in my car tires here and there over the years. Most of the time I wasn't even aware I had one until a mechanic pointed it out to me. Or until my wife said, "Hey, Leemie, your car looks like it's slumped over to one side. Are you sure your tires are okay on the right?" Okay, so she's the mechanical one in the family.

Slow leaks are sneaky. They're so subtle that because you don't notice them, they can blindside you. You go into the 7-Eleven to grab milk for dinner and come out to a tire that's hissing like a mad cat, then goes totally flat. Or what looks like a small bump in the road can cause the slow leak to become a hole, and you're left in the boonies on a country road.

Blowouts are no fun, but at least they're over with quickly. Your tire makes a loud *pop*, and even if you're not a brain scientist, you know to pull over to the shoulder. Then, if you're like me, you do the smart thing—you call roadside assistance and bask in the sun until they arrive.

When it comes to parenting powerful children, most parents choose the slow-leak method. They handle each situation with trepidation as it comes along, trying to keep the tire in good enough condition to keep trucking along.

But the slow-leak theory is doomed for failure. Most parents choose it because of a lack of confidence; they're not sure what they should do, and they're afraid to make a mistake.

The mistake would be not to act. You don't take on a powerful child in bits and pieces. You need to have a full box of tools at your disposal. That's what *Parenting Your Powerful Child* is about. It's the toolbox you'll need to fix and then redirect this powerful child you love so dearly.

Forced blowouts with your powerful child will not be pretty. But if you are decisive and you plan for them, you will make great headway with that child. That's because you, smart parent, are thinking through the strategies you're going to use ahead of time and how you're going to draw the parameters of the new behavior in your home.

The mistake would be not to act.

Some kids are so powerful that even when you're doing the right thing, they'll give you a run for your money. They don't like the idea you're on the right track. It's what I call "the fish out of water syndrome." When you hook a fish, he does something unnatural. He leaves the water—his comfort zone—and leaps right into the air, trying to shake that hook. Your kid will do the same thing, so expect the fight. But don't give up on your strategy, and don't fight back. Fighting is an act of cooperation, so don't cooperate with your child in that way. She's adept at needlessly drawing you into her hassles and battles.

Other kids will throw this line your way: "Go ahead and take away my car privileges. I don't care." That's an indication of how powerful those kids are. The reality is, they do care. They care deeply. The idea of having no car privileges freaks them out because it will change their entire lifestyle. However, they don't want you to know you're on the right track, so they pretend indifference.

So, long and short, if your kid starts to fuss or tosses you the "it doesn't matter" line, you can smile. You're already starting to win the game.

But you can't win the game if you don't play.

Let's be honest. Some kids are easy kids. They do what they're told. They obey. They're predictable. You can count on them. You don't even have the dreaded toddler tantrums or the ripples that many parents face with their teenagers. Life with those children is a stroll on Easy Street, so to speak.

Then there's your powerful child.

I ought to know. I was one of them, even though no psychologist back then would have thought to call me that. But my mother, God rest her soul, was a saint. She of all people would have had the right to give up on her juvenile-acting son, but she didn't. I'm thankful she lived long enough to see me make something of myself, because she, one of my high school teachers, and my wife-to-be all believed that I could take

> **You can't win the game if you don't play.**

my innate power skills and use them to entertain and help people form rock-solid families. Am I still juvenile-acting? I admit that my buddy Moonhead and I have been known to wrestle each other—to our wives' dismay—as we wait for a table at our local restaurant.

Hardly anyone—other than those three ladies—expected me to make anything of myself. Yet here I am today.

You, parent, are your child's best champion. Powerful kids don't just happen; they're created . . . by you.

The good news is, what you've done, you can undo with determination, persistence, and willpower.

Powerful Ideas That Work

My youngest daughter has given me a run for my money since the day she was born. She was the toddler who stared me in the eye and pushed Cheerios off her plate and onto the floor. I swear, she just wanted a reaction. When she was 5, I told her to stay in the yard and not go out onto the street. Two minutes later, I heard cars honking, and there she was—in the middle of the street, standing there!

Now she's 11, and I can't count how many times my heart has stopped with this kid. Three months ago, when I was at my wits' end with her, I heard you speak on a radio program, and it gave me an idea. The next time she pulled an attention-getting stunt, I was ready. The timing was perfect. My husband had planned to take the three girls on a father-daughter campout weekend, and they were leaving early the next morning. Julie was really mad she didn't get to go. She slammed a couple doors, but I didn't react. She turned on the tears and yelled, "You're so unfair!" She spent the whole next day in her room, refusing to eat. She thought she was punishing me, but I had a nice, quiet day I really needed, and I slept soundly because I knew we'd done the right thing.

The next day she tried a few more power plays, but I remained calm. I turned my back and settled in on our sunporch to read. By the third day, she said to me meekly, "Uh, Mom, could you and I do lunch? I'll help." I was stunned. She even helped with the dishes. And when her sisters came home that evening, she was nice to them and asked about their trip. She hugged my husband. Then she turned to me and said, "Mom, thanks for having lunch with me." Because I stuck to my guns and used your advice, I have an adolescent that I now not only love but also like.

Jessica, Ohio

Power Points

- Powerful kids don't just happen; they're created.
- Give in and you won't win.
- Force a blowout, then remain calm.

2

Power Comes in Different Packages

Your personal power source is right under your nose . . . and she's workin' ya.

I live in the Arizona desert, and we have these little creatures called desert rats. They're everything you think a rat might be. They have long tails and they'll eat anything. And I do mean anything.

I have an Audi convertible. Those rats had the entire desert to choose from, and one decided to nest in the engine of my Audi. Then, one evening, it devoured for an early dinner some wires that were part of my transmission. It was so adept at getting into the small, hidden places that the Audi dealership had to pull the entire transmission to oust it.

Now, I'm no mechanic, so I didn't understand the mechanical aspects of everything those talented men had to do. But I did understand the bill.

Really well, in fact. It had a three, a one, a zero, another zero, and some change. If you're still with me on the math, that little rat cost me $3,100. Not that I was ever a lover of rats to start with, but I really don't like them now, because they hit me where it hurts—in the pocketbook.

One little rat had added up to one gigantic problem, because it short-circuited my car's transmission.

I'm no electrician either, but I do know that crossed wires create a short, and that red and black wires are different and need to be separated. A simple short can take a whole building down; it can knock out an entire neighborhood's power.

So it is with your powerful child. One powerful kid can add up to a gigantic problem, because that child creates shorts that impact your entire family's transmission.

You know what I mean. You have your feet up on the couch one night, anticipating a peaceful evening. Then your powerful child turns your living room into a war zone with one look or comment.

If you think of which child in your family has the ability to do that, in an instant you've identified your powerful child. Every family has one, but it's not always who you think.

Power comes in different packages, but they all add up to the same thing—manipulating and controlling you. And those kids are masters at it.

The Loud, Aggressive Manipulator

There's no doubt this kid is powerful. You can't miss him—he's loud, obnoxious, and aggressive. He's the one who loudly proclaims any need or desire and ramps up his request with any vocal method possible until his request is met. He's the one who won't let you have a single phone conversation without an interruption. He's also the one who's most likely to become a bully on the school playground because he likes to boss people around.

Ryan was a loud kid from the instant he was laid on his mother's chest. He cried loudly as an infant, and he was aggressive as a 3-year-old toward his baby brother. He wanted no part of this new package delivered to their home, so he ramped up his powerful behavior. When he was 9, a teacher caught him running down the block after he threw a rock through the front window of her home, and she marched him to his home. When asked why he did it, Ryan proclaimed, "Because I felt like it."

The Temperamental Manipulator

We've all seen them. The 2-year-old screaming in his stroller at the mall because his father won't stop at the play area. The 3-year-old who pitches a fit at the grocery store when his mom won't buy him the candy he wants. The 5-year-old who doesn't want to leave the Y, so he launches a full throwing-himself-on-the-ground fit at the poolside, in full view of the entire Y's occupants.

If your kid is throwing temper tantrums at ages 2, 3, and 5, he's still going to be throwing them at age 8 unless you do something about it. He'll also be throwing them at age 17, only they'll look a little different. He's going to be calling you names you didn't realize he knew, stealing your money, and borrowing your car without permission.

A distraught mom wrote me last week. "I don't understand," she said. "I've always given Sandra everything she could ever want. You'd think she could show a little appreciation. But when I give her one thing, she always wants more." Moms, you in particular are often compassionate people who want everybody to feel good. You want to please your child and make her path in life smooth. But if you do so, you're actually hurting her by cushioning her from reality and the consequences of her choices. How many friends will she keep if she's considered a temperamental witch by her peers? If she's an unpredictable person who could turn on anyone at any minute and demand that others do things for her?

Kids get powerful early, and they will become harder to deal with if they're allowed to progress in their behavior. That's why there's no better time than the present to change your strategy.

The Curveball Manipulator

This is the late-bloomer child who seems to go from manatee to werewolf overnight. She's always been a mellow, easygoing, co-operative kid who adheres nicely to the parental program. Then hormones ignite a personality you didn't know existed. But don't let go of your parental control at this point; it's too critical for your sake and your child's. She needs to be dealt with immediately. You need a game plan. (For additional help on your specific issues, consult my book *Have a New Teenager by Friday*.)

Adolescence (I define this as ages 11 to 19 years old) and pre-adolescence (when your daughter has nothing to train but she wants a training bra, and your son is starting to look for hair on his private parts) are a necessary evil in life that kids have to go through. Every child is affected by adolescence differently because of the physiological, psychological, and hormonal changes going on. Hormones can become the spark that ignites a fire, which then explodes. All of a sudden the kid you never thought you'd have a problem with becomes a defiant, rebellious handful.

Ann was a happy-go-lucky child who was known for singing and creating plays for her family. She had the kind of innocent, joyful spirit that made everyone around her smile. Then, at age 10, she got her first period. By age 11, she had become surly, argumentative, and hard to get along with. She cried every day she had to go to school, and when she wasn't crying, she was screaming at her parents, who were completely floored by this change in their child and didn't know how to deal with it. As a result, Ann's behavior continued for two years, until they at last were forced to seek medical and psychological help.

Jared went from a straight-A kid at age 13 to a sloppy, disorganized, not-caring kid who rarely finished his homework at age 14.

Your manatee-to-werewolf transition may not be as abrupt as Ann's or Jared's, but I bet anything you're thinking, *God, please make this kid 25 . . . tomorrow.*

The curveball manipulator is the kid who leaves his parents scratching their heads at night. He's hard to figure out because he swings from one extreme to the other and sometimes lands in the middle. One day he might be a real human being. The next day, nothing is ever good enough, life's unfair, and you're unfair. He's high-maintenance and exhausting. If he could be registered on a seismogram, he'd look like an image of Southern California . . . on a bad day.

> I bet anything you're thinking, *God, please make this kid 25 . . . tomorrow.*

The Quiet, Shy Manipulator

These children are often not identified as powerful children, but they can be the most powerful of all. They hold all the cards because by their silence, they force you to extract information from them. You don't know what they're thinking.

"My son is really shy," a woman told me when I was in private practice. She apologized because her 6-year-old son wouldn't come out from behind her to meet me. He had a death grip on the back of her jeans. She'd come to see me because she was concerned about the fact that her child only wanted her and didn't want to interact with any kids his own age. She'd already held him back a year from starting school and wondered what to do about the next year.

As I talked with the woman, I watched the boy's behavior. The kid was a master manipulator, and he wasn't even in kindergarten yet. He had his mama wrapped around his pinkie. He was the one in control. When he decided it was time to go, he tugged on his mom's behind.

She said automatically, "Oh, he wants to go."

I stopped her. "But is that what you want? Didn't you come here to find a solution to what's happening with your son?"

She looked confused, as if she'd never thought of her own needs. "Well, he gets antsy if I talk too long."

I looked her straight in the eye. "I wasn't asking about him; I was asking about you. You say your son is shy, but he's using that shyness to control you, your schedule, and your behavior."

Her jaw dropped.

You see, at 6 years old, that boy had his mother figured out, and she was falling for it hook, line, and sinker. Of course he didn't want to interact with anyone else, because his mama did everything for him. She was predictable; he could control her. Easy as pie.

So when I suggested otherwise, he first pulled out the bucket of tears. When that scenario didn't work, he got angry. I had to put the cajoling mother outside the door in order to even work with the kid.

Children who learn how to be quiet, shy controllers grow up to be quiet, shy controllers.

Like 14-year-old Janelle, who gives her mom the silent treatment every day on the way home from school and then jabbers for five hours on the phone with her friends. But when she wants something from her mom or dad, she can be utterly charming.

> **That boy had his mother figured out, and she was falling for it hook, line, and sinker.**

Or 21-year-old Richard, who is still jobless because he can't find the courage to do a job interview and spends the day hanging out in his bedroom in his parents' basement, playing warfare games on his computer. And what does his mom do? She does his laundry and serves him dinner downstairs so he doesn't have to interrupt his game.

You think those kids don't have the upper hand? Indeed, they're milking their parents for all they're worth.

The Sensitive, Walk-on-Eggshells Manipulator

Do you walk on eggshells because you want to make sure you don't upset your "sensitive" son or daughter, because then they'll create a scene?

Parents get sucked into the "sensitive" child. They tell me, "Oh, Dr. Leman, he's so sensitive." They see it as a virtue.

The parent continues. "If I say anything to correct him, he immediately cries and says, 'I'm no good.'"

Of course the kid does. He's a master manipulator.

What he wants his mother to say is, "Now, now, honey, Mommy didn't want that. Forgive me for saying that." Then he wants her to placate him for doing her parental job—trying to hold him accountable for his actions.

Many parents today just want their kids to be happy. But are you always happy? Is being happy what pays the bills and makes the world go round?

These kids who are "sensitive" are actually very powerful little buzzards. They are tyrants who grow up to be adult tyrants. Think of the marriage where the woman turns on her tears to bring her husband to his knees so he'll agree with something she wants to do—even when he doesn't think it's wise—because he can't stand to see his wife cry. He never ends up telling her what he thinks, because he walks on eggshells around his "sensitive" wife. Or the reverse—the woman who is married to the "sensitive" man who has to have dinner served at a certain time or his temper explodes.

> **Many parents today just want their kids to be happy. But are you always happy?**

Where do you think those adults learned their controlling behaviors? In their home when they were growing up.

What is a sensitive child really saying? "I'm going to make you toe the line. You will approach me the way I want to be approached, or I'll throw a big fit and make you sorry."

And parents fall for it.

I remember talking to a 5-year-old when I was in private practice. The kid would talk softer and softer until you could hardly hear her. That forced me, as an adult, to sit on the edge of my chair and get closer and closer to the kid to hear what she was going to say. I finally said, "You're trying to get Dr. Leman on the floor, aren't you?"

She flashed a grin. "Yeah."

Kids are manipulative. They know they can make you kowtow to them, so that's what they do. If you raise your voice or say something your child doesn't want to hear, what happens? She cries. She throws a temper tantrum, then yells, "You hate me." And with the flourish of a top actress, she flings herself on the bed and spouts, "You don't love me!"

But don't fall for that powerful little sucker who uses her "sensitivity" and that disappointed, forlorn look to get what she wants. She's workin' ya.

The Stubborn, Procrastinating Manipulator

This is the child who refuses outright to do what you asked, doesn't respond, or puts off the task as long as possible, until hopefully you'll forget you even asked. These kids are annoying and frustrating because you can't count on them. They're also high-maintenance because you always have to be on their case about something.

"Is your homework done?"

"Did you take out the garbage?"

You're always asking because you never know if they have accomplished a task or not. After all, they've got to get their homework done, right? And if you miss a garbage pickup, your garage might get rather aromatic.

But if they didn't accomplish those tasks, what would really happen?

They'd have to come up with a good excuse on their own for failing to do their homework (and teachers aren't stupid, contrary to their students' opinion).

One missed garbage pickup isn't the end of the world. Even better, perhaps a bag or two of it would make a nice addition to your child's bedroom for the next week. Bet he wouldn't forget again.

The stubborn kid is saying, "You're not going to make me do it. I'm in charge here."

The procrastinating manipulator is saying, "I'm going to do what I want when I want. I'm in charge here."

Your job is to make sure that what happens next is a losing proposition—for your child.

Power That Serves a Purpose

Chances are, you haven't said the word *purposive* today. You probably haven't said it this week, this month, or even this year. It's not a word most people use. But it's an important one for you to know.

Powerful, attention-getting behavior is *purposive*, meaning it serves a purpose.

All kids are attention-getters. They're crafted to crave connection and attention. Some will do it by getting good grades in school, pleasing their parents, or being helpful around the house. Others get it by driving you crazy with their antics so that you have to pay attention.

Kids who start off as attention-getters and don't receive attention in a positive way will then focus on getting it in a negative way. Take me, for example. I had a perfect older sister and a big brother I thought was close to perfect. I was the little cub who couldn't measure up. So instead of excelling in school like them, I became the class clown. Sure, I got attention—lots of it—but it was the negative kind, where people shook their heads and muttered under their breath, "Poor May Leman. To have a kid like that . . ."

Notice that whether the attention is positive or negative, it's still attention. But if the kid continues to feel discouraged about a lack of attention and thinks, *This isn't the way life should be*, he will become even more powerful. The older your kid becomes, the higher the ability he has to make you pay attention to him.

> **Chances are, you haven't said the word *purposive* today.**

Kids are perceptive, even at an early age. They size up the social milieu they're growing up in. If a parent is antsy and picks up an infant at her first whimper, what will the kid end up doing? Get behind that infant's eyes for a minute. Would you rather lie by yourself or be rocked on your mom's hip? Be next to those sterile, cool sheets in your crib or nestled between those nice, cozy, warm pillows, close to your mom's heart?

If you parents overreact to something simple, like the elimination of bodily fluids and wastes, a powerful kid says to himself, *My parents are sure big on this, aren't they?* The smart kid will use that as an edge. It's no wonder so many parents wrestle through the potty-training phase. Does someone give you juice and a cookie every time you go poop? Then you shouldn't give that to your son or daughter either.

Through trial and error, if you reward a behavior long enough, it becomes ingrained behavior. Psychologists call it *operant conditioning*.

Kids learn to be powerful. Why? Because that power serves a purpose. It keeps the child moving forward. It builds a case: *I'm more important than anyone else in this family*. It reinforces the child's power grid. It puts him in the offense seat—it clarifies his reasoning that the best defense is a good offense. So the kid is always on the offensive. Purposive behavior makes your child feel like he's in control; he's the boss, with everybody else at his beck and call.

When your powerful kid is misbehaving, whether quietly or loudly, he has a goal in mind that serves his purpose. Guess who taught him the ropes? You. Yes, you. That powerful child has been watching you.

Think of Yourself as a Circuit Breaker

Remember the little desert rat that caused the expensive repair of my Audi? Just because it caused a short in the transmission wires?

To state it bluntly, you've got your own little rat to deal with, and you need to be the mechanic who not only fixes the short in the wires but also acts as the circuit breaker. Your child's power surge will only continue if she has easy access to the power source. You, parent, are that power source. And your kid knows how to push your buttons to gain your attention and at least some kind of control over her own life.

After all, you're the one who makes all the decisions for the kid. Or at least she thinks you do. That means you hold the power.

One woman told me, "No matter what I say to my son and daughter, they battle me on it. They always have to have the last word. It's so exasperating."

Perhaps they always have to have the last word because you have to have the first word. Ever think of it that way? That puts those daily battles with your child in a whole new light, now doesn't it?

Why would a kid still whine at age 10? Or throw temper tantrums at age 13? Because those behaviors have paid off.

Power comes in different packages, but they all hold something in common. Kids act the way they do because it works.

But we're going to change all that. Just wait and see.

Powerful Ideas That Work

Sally's a kind, honest kid who always does the right thing. At least I thought so until a week after her sixteenth birthday, when I got a phone call from the cops that she'd been caught breaking into someone's house.

I beat myself up. *You're such a bad mom. You must have done something wrong, or she wouldn't be like this.* Then I decided I had to get tough and stay tough. I did what you suggested. I arranged with the police to let her stay in jail for a few hours before I came to the station to pay her fine. I took away her driving privileges since she'd used them wrongly. I drove her to court, but I didn't sit with her. I sat at the back of the room and let her be the one to answer to the judge for her actions. Facing the consequences and stressing out about what would happen to her when she faced the judge was a reality check she needed.

Kara, Texas

Power Points

- All kids are attention-getters. If they can't get attention positively, they'll get it negatively.
- All powerful behavior serves a purpose.
- If you have the first word, your child will have to have the last word.

3

The Loud, Aggressive, Temperamental, Curveball Manipulator

*This powerful child is easy to spot—
you can hear him from across the yard.
So can your elderly neighbors.*

Brent is the most obnoxious kid in his entire fifth-grade class. He was also the most obnoxious kid in his second-grade, third-grade, and fourth-grade classes. All that to say Brent hasn't changed much over the years. He's the youngest of four stair-step boys, and it's clear he doesn't get any attention at home, so he goes overboard in seeking it—negatively—at school. He has to be the first one to the door of the classroom when the bell rings, so he'll knock other kids out of the way to slide there first. He makes nasty comments to those who are of a different race than he is and has earned three forced vacations from school as a result. If he doesn't agree with something another kid says, he gets right in that kid's face—I'm talking an inch away—and loudly proclaims his opinion. During math class, he interrupts other students and starts to debate them. When the teacher tells him he can't interrupt and begins to explain that his reasoning is incorrect, he interrupts her and tells her that he knows better.

Is it surprising that the instant Brent opens his mouth, his classmates roll their eyes? Or that teachers start to get a little red-faced and discuss the next "Brent saga" in the teachers' lounge over lunch? Or that next year's math teacher has already decided to retire early so she won't have him as a student?

Yet his mother went to the principal, wringing her hands, and complained, "My son doesn't have any friends. He's so unhappy."

Oh, really? And who would want to be friends with that kind of a kid?

Mama Bear is defending her cub when what her cub needs is a wake-up call, a cold dose of reality about his behavior toward others. What she needs is to spend time with her annoying little cub, instead of shopping 24-7 to get away from all the boisterous cubs in her den.

Then there's Sadie, who's as temperamental as they come. Her feelings are always hurt . . . or on the way to being hurt. Her whine can be heard across three tables in the lunchroom. She's quick to drum up tears for sympathy. Her conversation is all about herself. She's always talking about her older sister and what a pain in the neck her little brother is. Her language is very babyish for a 12-year-old. It's no wonder that she changes from friend group to friend group. Other kids can only take her in small doses.

And there's Casey—the good kid gone bad. At least that's what his aunt says. From an A– or B+ student who helped out his grandma after school at age 13, to a smokin', drinkin', cussin' tough guy who got caught setting a fire behind a local business at age 15. He's running with a completely different crowd—one his parents don't approve of at all. They can't figure out where they went wrong, and they feel helpless to rein Casey in. It's never entered their minds that he can't legally drive alone in their state yet, and that they have the almighty parental power concerning whether he uses their vehicle or not. When you can't get somewhere, it's hard to get into the kind of trouble he's getting into.

> **Who would want to be friends with that kind of a kid?**

The loud, aggressive, temperamental, curveball manipulators are the easiest of all powerful kids to spot. That's because they are loud, aggressive, and temperamental and throw you huge curveballs. But they're probably the most insecure of all the power-driven kids, which is why they're trying so hard. They fear they'll be lost in the shuffle—at school or at home—if they're not always recognized. They are attention-seeking junkies, to put it mildly.

Like 9-year-old Noah, who has to be the leader of his group. If anyone even suggests the group plays something other than their usual activity, he first tries to strong-arm the other kid. If that doesn't work, he goes off and sulks. And if that doesn't work, he incites a fight so he can get the playground monitor involved and ruin everyone's playtime.

When powerful kids don't get what they want, they ramp it up to the next level.

All they're doing is playing you.

The Loud and Aggressive Kid

"You can't make me do it!"

"He deserved it, so I hit him back!"

"Like you're perfect!"

All of these are cookie-cutter statements that a loud, aggressive, attention-seeking, powerful child would say. Often they will be followed by some body poses and hand gestures that you might not find appropriate.

These kids love to argue, and they'll look for a fight. But don't give it to them. If you cave in and fight back, you're giving them exactly what they want—a good duel. To ensure they'll get one next time, they'll up the ante.

To these kids, it doesn't matter who is around and sees their behavior. They're not embarrassed if Aunt Millie sees them arguing with you, or even if the old lady across the street does. They're in the fight for the moment—and to win. They're in control. *Look at me*, they're thinking. *I'm throwing Mom's whole world upside down right now. Now that's power.*

How do you know if you have a powerful kid? Check your own reaction to his behavior: "You can't do that to me," you spout. "I'm your *mother*." Then the stomach acids start churning, and you have to dig for the Rolaids.

If your kid's behavior provokes that kind of emotional response—and it ain't pretty—that's a good indicator your kid has developed some power. If you powerfully up the ante in your response, your child takes it as a challenge to top your play. Thus begins the power struggle, with neither side winning and your relationship suffering.

Chances are, in any fight, you're going to lose. That's because you have far more to lose than he does. You care what Aunt Millie thinks; he couldn't give a rat's tail what she thinks. All he knows is that she gives him lame hand-knitted scarves every Christmas.

And after all, since he's a kid (unless he's old enough to look like a man), people will give him a pass. They'll shake their heads at his behavior and say, "Oh, boys can be so raucous." They'll give him the eagle eye for a second, thinking, *What is wrong with that kid?*

But trust me, they'll take a longer look at you, parent, and here's what they'll think: *What is wrong with that parent? To raise an obnoxious kid like that?*

So here's what you do. You look at the other people in the room or the mall and say, "Well, some people's children," and you step over the tantrum-throwing youngster or walk away from the yelling teenager.

> **How do you know if you have a powerful kid? Check your own reaction to his behavior.**

A loud and aggressive kid will go to great lengths to show you how powerful he is. That's why you need to step over the kid psychologically and not let him get to you. If your child starts shouting something inappropriate, you might calmly say, "I'm sure that's the way you see it, but I don't see it that way at all." And you disengage from the conversation.

Kids who throw tantrums (whether physical or verbal ones) are usually angry and frustrated. That's because many of these kids are perfectionists. When life doesn't go well or the way they want it to go, or they make a mistake, or someone doesn't do exactly what they expected, they fall apart.

In their minds, it's a terrible thing to make a mistake.

Many of these kids have grown up in homes where, when a drink spilled or a cup broke, it was a big deal. There was a verbal lashing for carelessness, a berating about things that cost money, and a putting down for the kid being such a putz. That's because with a perfectionistic kid, there's usually also at least one perfectionistic parent around.

That's why you, parent, can make such a big difference. Things won't always go as planned. Cups will break. Drinks will spill. It's not the end of the world. You get a rag, dustpan, and broom, and life goes on. There's no need for a berating. The way you respond even to the little things in life has everything to do with how your child will respond.

What you can do

- Resist the powerful temptation to fight back.
- Step over the kid psychologically and go on your way.

The Temperamental Kid

A 10-year-old doesn't still whine unless it works to serve her purposes, does she?

The temperamental kid is unpredictable, except for the fact that she's predictably mercurial. Anything can set her off. She's a woe-is-me, everything-is-against-me kind of person, and the mood swings aren't only due to pubescent or adolescent hormones. They're a learned behavior.

Kids who are allowed to get away with temperamental behavior become adults who manipulate and control others through temper tantrums. They are immature people who will look like complete fools to the rest of the adult population, making a spectacle of themselves. They are self-absorbed and hedonistic because they are coddled too much by parents who want to smooth their paths in life.

If your kid says, "I'm no good" or "I didn't do a good job," you say, "Why, honey, that's not true. You did a great job." Or if your kid flings at you, "You don't love me!" you (especially moms) go out of your way to try to make things better: "Of course I love you. What would make you think I don't love you?" And the parental hand-wringing begins.

But those answers only validate the attention-seeking, powerful personality of your child. Instead, say, "Wow, I'm sorry you feel that way. I don't think that's true, but if you want to believe that, it's your right." I can guarantee you will get a surprised quirk of the eyebrows, because your kid will be trying to figure you out. That's because you didn't fall for "the plan" to coddle her and talk her out of her temperamental hissy fit.

When she says, "I don't feel like going," you say firmly, "There are times in life when I don't feel like going where you want me to take you either, but I still go."

When he complains, "That teacher drives me crazy. He assigns too much homework, and I can't get it all done," and then gives you the pout, hoping you'll help out, what should you say?

"You won't always like every teacher, but they're put on this earth to help you learn. And you're not the only one in the class who got the homework, are you?" Then turn your back and walk away. After all, whose homework is it?

Little things set off the temperamental kid. When he's distressed about something that isn't perfect, the best way to handle it is to say, "I know that's a big thing to you. But I gotta tell you, it's not to me. I think it looks great, but I know you don't. You can continue to think that if you wish, but I believe it's fine." Such an approach diminishes the probability of the temperamental kid going into high gear.

But if you respond the traditional way, piling on the praise—"Now, why do you say that? That's a really good model airplane"—you'll only gain the "No, it's not!" vehement statement, a slammed door, and tears. That's because the kid knows you don't understand, and he'll get himself all worked up. If he thinks it's bad, you telling him it's good won't accomplish any purpose.

What you can do

- Don't deny your kids' feelings, but provide a different, balanced perspective.
- Don't coddle. Your child needs to feel the consequences of his actions.
- Don't rescue. His work and activities are his work and activities.
- Use realistic, pragmatic straight talk to help him stay in second gear and not go to third gear.

One of the biggest responsibilities of a parent is to be that circuit breaker that controls all the power surges in the family. If you overreact (this is especially true of firstborns), your child will overreact. Little things that happen will become big things.

If you overreact . . . your child will overreact.

For you parents of young children, you have to know about a natural phenomenon: when kids get overtired, they're more likely to have a meltdown. I call it "the point of no return." Once you get to that point, you could be Sigmund Freud and Alfred Adler combined and have mastered every Kevin Leman book there is, but the kid won't wind down or calm down until he cries himself to sleep.

Some kids go with the flow. Others are like clockwork. If they don't get sleep, they're miserable, loud tyrants.

So if you agreed to have dinner at a friend's house an hour past your young child's bedtime, you're asking for a major fuss. You'll not only pay for it that night but the next day too—with a grouchy kid. But there's a great solution. It's called a babysitter.

For you parents of teenagers, let me give you a helpful suggestion. If you know of things that will upset your son or daughter, you see them coming, and you have a way of preventing them from happening without your teenager's knowledge, then do it. For example, let's say you have a fastidious teenage daughter who always lays out her school clothes for the next day on the chair in her bedroom. You notice that the cat has sneaked into her room while she's off rehearsing for a school play. You know she won't get home until after 10:30 p.m., and then she'll see all that cat hair on her sweater and flip out. So you, smart parent, get one of those sticky roller contraptions out of the drawer, and in 20 seconds the roller is full of cat hair and the sweater has none. Then you make sure that Bessie the cat is safely locked out of that bedroom.

Is that coddling your child? No, that's called grace and putting out fires before they start. But you don't do that all the time. Everybody needs a few road bumps in life to fine-tune their personality and to give them empathy for others.

The Curveball Kid

This kid really throws you for a loop. One minute it seems she's an agreeable kid, and the next you don't even recognize her as your child. There's no way to predict her behavior since she catches you completely off guard. One of life's unexplainable mysteries—poignantly painful to parents—is a child who goes along with the parental program with a smile on her face and seems to get along with everyone. Then, almost overnight, you begin to see signs that your child isn't who you thought she was.

Curveball kids can make swift downward spirals. That's why I urge parents to pay close attention to several things. First, sudden shifts—falling grades, a major personality change—are often the result of drug or alcohol use. Insist that your child get a drug test. If she is using drugs or alcohol, it's better for you to know sooner than later. If she isn't, just making her go in for the test—with you accompanying her—may provide the needed wake-up call that you are noticing her behavior. Second, use the history button on your child's computer to see what sites she's accessed recently. And third, check out her emails and her text messages. She may scream that doing so is a violation of her privacy, but she still lives under your roof, and your role as a parent is to get to the bottom of the situation.

With a curveball kid, what you're facing at this moment will only be the start of what you will face if you don't handle that child right now. The turning point for many curveball kids is how the parents respond when they get that phone call from the principal, the police station, or any other authority figure.

When you do get that call (and you will, with curveball kids), the best thing you can do is remain calm. Speak straightforwardly to your child and put the responsibility for the action in her court: "I feel bad about this situation. Why you did it and how you did it are going to be between you and the juvenile judge. I don't need to know all the details. But obviously I'm disappointed to know you got yourself in this situation. If I can help you in any way, I'd like to. But I'm not sure how I could, since I'm not the owner of that bag of meth and I wasn't caught snorting it."

It's a little reality therapy to throw your kid's way. What you're saying is that, on one hand, you feel bad for her. On the other hand, you sure hope she can work this out.

You continue. "Apparently you have to be in front of the judge on February 16. I have no idea what you're going to tell him. If I were 14, I think that would throw me for a loop. I'm sure you'll think of something. I'm just sorry you got yourself into this situation."

Then end the conversation, keeping the responsibility with your child.

If there's ever a teachable moment for your child, it will be when she stands in front of that judge—alone.

But many parents will never let it go that far. They will spend $8,000 on a lawyer who will get the charges dropped or swept under the rug. Parents don't want the indigestion, the negative PR, or the embarrassment.

However, let me guarantee you, it will only get worse the next time if you rescue your child this time.

Letting the judge's verdict be the reality discipline is your best option. He'll clearly explain what the unacceptable behavior is and why it's unacceptable, grill her as to why she made that choice, talk about what would be a better choice, and then sternly give the consequences not only of that event but of any further similar events. I don't know a first-time offender on the planet who hasn't stood with shaking knees before a judge.

What you can do

- Be alert to and research the reasons for the sudden shift in your child.
- Stay calm and logical.

- Put the ball on your child's side of the net.
- Don't rescue your child. Let reality do the talking.

Powerful Ideas That Work

When Shelli entered her junior year of high school, she fell in with a different crowd. All of a sudden she had to be cool. Her clothes changed to sexy ones, and she started to get sassy. Then one day she got into a fistfight with another girl and a cop escorted her home.

That night I went online and read some of your blogs about discipline. I decided to give her what you call "the bread-and-water treatment." A roof over her head and food to eat, but no spending money, no activities other than school. I drove her straight to school every day and picked her up five minutes after school was out.

It was three months of pure you-know-what for me (I'm a single mom) until she came around. I lost some work clients because of my new schedule, and things got tight financially. We're now on a baked potato and PB&J diet for a while, but my old Shelli is back. The sacrifice was worth it.

P.S. Funny how those popular friends disappeared when the cops showed up. That was a shocking lesson Shelli will never forget either.

Madeline, New York

————————— **Power Points** —————————

- No one wins a fight.
- Overreacting creates a powerful child.
- Coddling and rescuing create immature, temperamental, powerful children.
- Always respond logically and calmly.

4

The Quiet, Shy, Sensitive, Walk-on-Eggshells Manipulator

You may not recognize this child as powerful, but she quietly holds all the cards . . . until you decide to play your hand differently.

My middle daughter, Krissy, has always been sensitive. She has a sensitive nose like a beagle—she can smell things others can't. She has sensitivities to light and cloudy days.

But when parents tell me their child is sensitive, they're not talking about heightened physical senses. They're talking about something else. I immediately equate the word *sensitive* with *powerful*. They're telling me that they're stepping on eggshells because of their quiet, shy, sensitive child.

What they don't know is that their child is, in all probability, a powerful attention-getter who gets exactly what he wants from adults through the "poor me, I'm so shy and sensitive" act. If

Mom or Dad has a compassionate side, then one glimpse of such behavior and that parent will fall like an egg from a tall chicken. And grandparents? They're toast.

Because the quiet, shy, sensitive, walk-on-eggshells manipulators share so much in common, I'm addressing them together in this chapter.

Quiet and Shy—For Real or Learned?

Some children run silent and deep. They're simply quiet children by temperament, and they crave time alone, away from the hubbub of the rest of the world. One brilliant 13-year-old I know plays seven instruments—and well, I might add—draws and paints like a professional, and has a contract offered from

Some children run silent and deep.

a publisher for her first fantasy novel. But her best friends are not human; they're books and horses. Yet she's a well-balanced, respectful teenager who pitches in, helps at home even before she's asked, writes notes to her grandparents and a pen pal in Africa, and then retreats to her room for the quiet time she needs.

These aren't the type of kids I'm talking about in this chapter. I'm talking about the powerful kids who make you work hard to get something—anything—out of them. It's like pulling teeth. Quiet, shy, sensitive, walk-on-eggshells children get their psychological jollies by watching Mom or Dad jump through all kinds of hoops to get any information from them: how school was, what they liked about the school play or the movie they just saw, and so on.

So the parent hovers like a private investigator, asking questions and hoping for any shred of information.

The kid sits back, not saying a word, amused by the depth of the effort taken to get him to say anything.

The parent has nothing to bargain with, because the kid seems to hold all the aces. After all, you can't make a kid talk. You can't force him to share about his life. All you can do is . . . wait.

Questions, Questions . . .

If you have a quiet-by-temperament child who isn't a talker to begin with, does it make any sense at all to fire questions at him? All you'll get is grunts at best or an "I don't know."

What "I don't know" really means is "I'm not going to tell you." There's the power.

Don't you think your kid has an opinion of that day at school? Or the play or movie he saw?

Perhaps a neighbor takes your 10-year-old to a major league ball game, and afterward you pepper him with questions. You hear from your neighbor that they had a great time, but you want all the juicy details. If he's a powerful kid, he isn't going to say a word. Why should he? He develops a power base just by being quiet.

After all, he won't get in trouble for not talking. He can never be criticized or told what he says is wrong if he doesn't talk. So he becomes a kid of few words. That same kid will marry at age 24 and still be a man of few words who controls his home through his silence, unless something changes in your family on a daily basis that transforms the course of his journey in life.

Why do I say that? These are kids that parents spend a lot of time "shoulding" on: "You should do this." "You should do that."

If you were constantly being told what to do, would you always feel like answering? Would you *ever* feel like answering?

> **If you were constantly being told what to do, would you always feel like answering? Would you ever feel like answering?**

In the face of silence, we parents increase the attempt to get answers to our questions. "So . . . why don't you tell me about your day?" we cajole. We ask more questions, trying to draw the child out. We think we're helping, but all we're doing is making that child withdraw further. To stay in control, he can't afford to say anything, so he doesn't.

What you can do

- Go out of your way not to ask questions. Let silence reign. It's okay to be quiet, especially on the way to and from school.
- Decide that you're not going to do all the talking at the dinner table. If you don't always fill the air, sooner or later your kid will say something.
- When your kid does talk, say in a calm tone, "Tell me more about that." It may sound like a command, but such a comment doesn't put his defenses up. It says, "I'd like to know more. Tell me about your world."
- Realize that the times your child wants to talk might not be perfect timing for you. I had one daughter who wouldn't say much until she wanted to talk. And when she wanted to talk, she could talk your ear off. But it was often at inopportune times, like when I was beat and ready to hit the sack. She'd plop on my bedroom floor, start talking, and yak for an hour.

If your child is one of those kids who likes to climb under a rock and doesn't want to come out, could it be because you're circling that rock with a pitchfork in hand? From his point of view, anyway?

Your kid can outwait you every time.

But if you don't pepper him with questions, sooner or later he'll come out . . . at least to eat.

Certain things all kids will do, and eating is one of them.

Sensitive and Walking on Eggshells

Aaron, the dad of an 8-year-old, came to talk to me because he was troubled about his daughter. The school principal had called for the second time that month. His daughter had flipped out when she walked into her classroom and found a substitute there instead of her regular teacher. She had panicked and fled down the hallway. That was the first of many situations Aaron and his wife faced with their "sensitive" daughter. Clearly she was controlling their lives, and it was causing a lot of stress in their family. That girl had everybody in her life tiptoeing around, trying to keep the stick of dynamite from exploding.

Aaron picked his daughter up at the school, took her through the McDonald's drive-through, and then went to a local park to chat. He said, "Lucy, you can't act that way at school, or any-where. You can't control everything in life. There will be substitute teachers and things you won't like. You have to learn how to deal with them."

Aaron handled that situation calmly and perfectly well. You might think his daughter would calm down. But she was a powerful kid with an agenda to make sure that all adults who dealt with her realized it was her way or the highway. So his daughter stared at him, then started screaming. So loudly, in fact, that a nearby cop thought a crime was being committed and stopped by to check it out. Aaron was embarrassed beyond belief.

But if I could give a parenting award, I'd give it to Aaron, who did the right thing, kept his cool in a time of crisis, and said what needs to be said. In the long run, consistency and a calm attitude will win out. Rearing a child, as you know, parents, is an ongoing process.

What you can do

- Realize that your child's "sensitivity," her seeming inability to cope with life or any changes from the norm, and her helplessness are actually a power play. Trust me, she's not helpless. She has an agenda, and it's to put you in her service. She's a tyrant, and she'll continue to be as long as you allow her to. It's not healthy either for you or for her to play that game.

- Don't be overimpressed with tears. The next time your kid prematurely turns on the waterworks because she doesn't want to do something, grab her hand and say, "I know this is something you don't want to do, but we're doing it. Come on."

- Take control of the master manipulator.

- If you are married, make sure that you and your spouse are on the same page in the way you handle your eggshell child. Kids tend to find favor with one parent and then work their manipulation overtime on that parent. As a result, it puts the spouses on opposite ends of the spectrum and becomes divisive to the marriage and home. Don't let a "sensitive" kid become a roadblock to a healthy marriage.

- Alert Grandma and Grandpa to your efforts and ask for their help. Grandmas especially can be worked over by a sensitive child, and grandpas are a soft touch anyway. Giving them the heads-up is only fair to everyone.

Evan, a guy I consider to be a really wise father, once told his shy teenage daughter, "Shyness is actually the opposite of what people think. It's saying, 'I'm so special that I'm convinced that anytime I go anywhere, everybody stares at me.'"

That comment revolutionized her world. The kid who had previously used her shyness to keep from interacting with others began seeking out other kids who tended to hang back in the corners. The focus shifted from "me, me, me" to them and their interests.

That same daughter, 10 years later, is working full-time with an international agency that assists refugees of wars and natural disasters. Her father couldn't be prouder of the way she turned out.

Instead of allowing your quiet, shy, sensitive, walk-on-eggshells child to manipulate you and control your world, find ways to broaden her world and allow her to give to others.

You'll be glad you did.

Powerful Ideas That Work

Our daughter is shy and sensitive—good at art and music but not very comfortable around people. A month ago, my wife had to go on a business trip overseas for three weeks. Sarah is in second grade, so she was in school most of the time, but I took her to music lessons.

The first week, Sarah started fussing in the middle of the lesson. I took her out, calmed her down, and offered her a snack I had in the car. By then the lesson time was over. The same thing happened the next week. The teacher stayed calm but eyed me and said, "I think you might have a power issue going on."

I was shocked. Sarah acted fine when my wife was there, but I found out later my wife bribed her with treats and did things in a certain order. Sarah couldn't deal with anything different. That's when my wife and I talked by phone and agreed on a plan, and I looped in the music teacher.

The next week we walked into lessons as usual. When Sarah started fussing, I simply walked out the door and shut it. Sarah screamed, but the teacher continued with the lesson as if she wasn't crying. Five minutes later (I was around the corner where Sarah couldn't see me), the crying stopped, and the teacher calmly taught the lesson. When it was over, she opened the door and smiled at me. "We had a good lesson today," she said. Indeed we did! Best of all, my wife and I have stuck to this new plan, and we haven't had any further episodes.

Bob, Illinois

Power Points

- Shy and sensitive = power-driven.
- Don't ask questions. Say instead, "Tell me more about that."
- Your "helpless" child is not helpless. She has an agenda.

5

The Stubborn, Procrastinating Manipulator

*This child has a powerful MO and
a very good rationale for it.*

Eleven-year-old Jason is a stereotypical procrastinator. When his dad asks him to clean the garage, he looks up from his computer screen and says, "Yeah, sure, Dad." But he never does it.

When his mom tells him, "Make sure all your laundry is downstairs. I'm doing laundry today," he says, "Uh-huh." But he never does it.

Sixteen-year-old Sharon always has to be right. Even if she doesn't know anything about the subject. She stubbornly holds the line on anything she believes is her right. And she refuses to do anything she absolutely doesn't have to do.

Both of these kids have very powerful motives of operation, and right now they're in control.

The Stubborn Kid

When you have a stubborn kid in the family, you have a stubborn adult. Powerful kids have at least one powerful parent somewhere in the mix. Stubbornness begets stubbornness. For example, in our family, my wife, Sande, is the stubborn one. She doesn't seem to be stubborn, but she is. She'd admit to it too. Our daughter Hannah got her stubborn traits from her mother. They're both as sweet as you can imagine, but you can't win a logical argument with either of them—ever.

You don't ever do battle with a stubborn kid. You don't try to prove them wrong. You don't try to win. If you play the parental card of an authoritarian, trying to prove that it's your right as a parent to call the shots, you're only looking for trouble.

Kids who are stubborn have a high need to be right. So no matter what you tell them, you'll get resistance—that push-back that says, "Hey, I know better than you."

What doesn't work

- Reacting emotionally.
- Taking things personally.
- Getting angry.
- Combatting your child's argument with facts of your own.
- Blowing small statements out of proportion.
- Telling your child, "I'm your mother/father, and I know more than you."

What you can do

- Before you talk to your stubborn kid, find a way to lower his defenses.

- Approach him with your hands in your pockets or some other body pose that isn't threatening.
- Say right off the bat, "I may not know what I'm talking about, and I could be dead wrong on this, but . . ." Then slip your child the straight skinny.

How does this work? Let's say you see the weather report and know that it's going to be nearly freezing by 1:00 p.m. Your junior high daughter hates to wear a coat—it's not "cool." You know if you say anything, she'll give you the eye roll and the "I'll be fine, Mom," and be out the door, coatless. Demanding she wear her coat because it'll be cold only ensures she'll go out of her way not to wear one.

So you strategize in advance how to lower her defenses.

When she whips down the stairs to grab her usual bagel out of the toaster on her way out the door, you say something simple like, "Oh, Andrea, I might be wrong on this, but I thought the weatherman said it was going to be really cold by 1:00 today."

Instead of being an invitation to stubbornness, your words put the ball in your daughter's court. If you're not pressuring her, chances are good that she might grab that jacket on the way out the door. After all, you've raised a smart daughter with common sense. She merely sidesteps it when she doesn't want you to win.

Don't look for trouble. Meeting stubborn with stubborn only leads to chaos.

Even when your kid says something stupid, don't provoke a fight by trying to play your parental trump card. Just say calmly, "You probably know best, honey." He'll discover soon enough if he's wrong. You don't have to point out the possibility.

Most parents act like Don Quixote, charging at windmills—with the same result.

Give up your need to be right in order to have a relationship that will last a lifetime with your child.

The Procrastinator

Some kids are naturally poky. They get dressed slowly, they take 20-minute showers, they take four hours to do two hours' worth of homework, and they're the last person to leave the dinner table. They simply *dawdle*.

Other kids are naturally high-strung. They get their homework done in study hall or as soon as they get home. They're way ahead of the game and always worried about the next thing, whatever that thing is.

It should be obvious, but in the fracas of parenting, sometimes we forget. Kids are different. One isn't necessarily better than the other—just different. That's why your approach has to be different for each child. There's no such thing as doing things equally for your kids. There's only equal love for each of them.

So is your kid naturally poky, or does he have an agenda? If you have a kid who's a procrastinator, there is certainly a yellow flag and probably a red flag that at least one of his parents has a critical eye. Of all the variables that affect personality and birth order, a critical-eyed parent can be one of the most destructive. If you want your kid to stop procrastinating, take a good look at yourself and your spouse (if you're married) or your ex (if you're divorced).

> **Is your kid naturally poky, or does he have an agenda?**

Who is the critical parent? The one who knows exactly how life should be? Who can look at a set of numbers and immediately know which one is wrong? Who will notice that a framed picture isn't hanging perfectly straight?

You know who you are, parent. Your expectations for your kid are so high and pressured that he's formed a defense mechanism—procrastination.

This is your child's way of protecting himself from your critical words. He's thinking, *If I don't finish this task, how can I be evaluated? It's not done yet. So I can't fail.*

Let's go back to Jason, from the beginning of this chapter, whose dad told him to clean the garage and he never did. When his dad ragged on him about it, he said, "Well, I started, and I'll finish it tomorrow."

> **He's thinking, *If I don't finish this task, how can I be evaluated? It's not done yet. So I can't fail.***

It's a lie he's telling himself. He's going to make his dad push him—and at great cost to Jason, his dad, and their relationship. His dad might as well save the effort and take the pressure off everybody by cleaning the garage himself, because it's never going to happen otherwise.

That's because Jason knows that no matter how well he does, his dad is going to "should" on him. He's going to tell Jason 10 different ways he should have improved on the job if he even dares to start it.

That's why your child procrastinates. He's his own worst enemy. He'll never accomplish anything if he's afraid of criticism. He'll never try if he's afraid of failing.

That's also why he appears discouraged—because he is. He thinks he can't live up to expectations—either his own or others', and most especially yours. If he doesn't try anything, he won't be held responsible for anything. So he spins his wheels and wastes time. He never invests his best efforts, because avoidance is better than facing the possibility of criticism or failure.

Let me ask you: Who is the organ grinder and who is the monkey?

Your child is great at getting around the rules. All he has to do is plead innocence or ignorance. Even though he doesn't seem to be disrespectful, he's actually being very disrespectful of the family's rules. But he does it in such a quiet way that you don't pick up on how powerful he is.

Problem is, if he's supposed to do something around the house, he'll make all sorts of promises. "Okay, Mom, I'll do it." Yet that task never gets done. Your kid gives you a lot of lip service, holding you at bay.

But the bottom line is that he still does what he wants to do.

What you can do

- If you're big on finding flaws, dial down your flaw picking. It's one of the most destructive things you can do in your relationship with your kids.
- Instead of heaping on praise, use realistic encouragement.

Praise focuses on the child himself: "Oh, you're the best kid in the world! You washed the kitchen floor and took the garbage out." Or "What a great kid. You took your sister to her sporting event." But is that really what you want to imply? Your kid isn't dumb. He knows you're lying. He's not the best kid in the world. There's a whole lineup in front of him.

Wouldn't you rather realistically encourage your kid by saying, "Wow, the room looks nice. Thanks for all your hard work." Or "Your concert was tremendous. I know you were worried about hitting that high note, but all that practice you did last week paid off. You have to feel really great about your performance." Notice that the comments focus on the work, not the person. That's the difference between praise and encouragement.

So be matter-of-fact. Thank your child for their effort.

Become the "Guard All"

Years ago there was a television ad for Gardol—an ingredient in Colgate toothpaste that kept plaque and other bad things away from your teeth. It featured a guy on a stage driving golf balls into a clear Plexiglas screen, and they bounced right off that screen.

Your kids, too, need a Gardol—some established limits that you put on family activities and pressures to guard against the frustration of overextending yourself and your kids to please others.

Just because the local dance school thinks your child is so talented that she should be in all five performances this year, does it mean she should be?

As soon as you receive the news, you call your sister and your best friend and the head of the PTA and say, "You're not going to believe this, but the top dance academy just called, and they want Shayla to be in all five concerts. Can you imagine? I'm so pleased."

And what do most parents say, especially moms? "Oh, that's wonderful!"

Parents tend to get sucked into the "my kid has to be the best" philosophy. And it's as addictive as crack cocaine. What parent doesn't want the chance to rave about Little Schnooky? But is all that activity really good for Little Schnooky—and for Mom and Dad?

You need to become the Gardol—the one who watches the demands and expectations on your children and who is respectful of their time. Many stubborn and procrastinating kids may simply be overscheduled. They need downtime, and they know the only way to get it is just not to do something. So they actively procrastinate.

If you're going to protect your little cub from the onslaught of opportunities, you need to develop what I call "*no* power." Over the years, we've had black power, brown power, and green power (which I call "economic power"), but women especially need to develop the *no* power to be able to say in a healthy way, "No, we're not going to be doing that this year."

> **Parents tend to get sucked into the "my kid has to be the best" philosophy.**

Don't guilt yourself into stacking the family schedule.

Don't be overly impressed with your own children or their abilities.

Don't be overly saturated with programs and activities. My rule is one activity per child per semester.

Instead, pay attention to your kid's heart.

Powerful Ideas That Work

Like father, like son. My 17-year-old son, Bryan, is as stubborn as my ex. Anytime I ask him to help out around the house, I get the brush-off. Or the "I'm busy right now. I'll do it later" thing. But he could spend all day working on the old car his dad helped him buy.

Then one day I heard you talk about stubborn, procrastinating kids. I put my plan into action. I didn't ask Bryan for anything for a whole week, and I didn't do anything for him either. By the end of the week, his laundry was piled up, and there were no leftovers in the fridge to grab. He was looking a little puzzled. He came in while I was making a salad for myself and said, "Uh, Mom, do you need help with anything?" I almost laughed out loud. Your suggestions really work.

P.S. Bryan found out he could cook. And yesterday he even took my car in to have the oil changed, without me asking. Blow me down. . . .

Janice, New Mexico

Power Points

- Where there's a stubborn kid, there's a stubborn adult.
- Strategize, then slip your kid a commercial announcement.
- Give up your parental need to be right. A relationship is far more important.
- Watch your critical eye. Lavish on realistic encouragement.

6

What Do Genes Have to Do with It?

Check out the personalities in the nursery, and you can predict what each kid will be like in 5, 10, 15 years.

When our firstborn, Holly, was 18 months old, we took a trip to Laguna Beach, California. Sande and I were excited to enlarge her world with her first experience at the beach—all that sand and the rolling waves to play in, with seashells to hunt. But after Holly's first tentative touch on the ground, she discerned that sand stuck to her fingers and insisted it be removed. Sande dutifully wiped Holly's hands clean. Our firstborn quirked a brow and pointed to the two remaining grains of sand on her hand. And her look said, "Uh, what exactly do I do with this stuff?"

At less than 2 years old, Holly was already forming her personality, which would have a lot to do with the direction her life would go. She was the kind of kid who liked all her ducks in a precise row. She was also good at managing others—whether her siblings wanted to be managed or not—and at multitasking, something I'm still to this day trying to accomplish.

Everyone is born with a unique temperament and personality. That's why I love observing babies in nurseries. If you watch for a few minutes, you'll see the personalities start to emerge. You can actually predict what that kid will be like in 5 years, 10 years, even 15 years. All kinds of studies have been done by researchers who look at babies in cribs in hospital nurseries and make predictions based on the kids' behaviors and demeanors.

> **Everyone is born with a unique temperament and personality.**

But it doesn't take a researcher to point out the obvious.

Some babies lie there quietly, casually taking in the room and its occupants. They're not bothered by the other crying babies. They seem to take things in stride.

Other babies are high-strung, crying and flinching at every noise. For them, getting out of the nursery and to a quiet place will be a dream come true. They're the ones who will need massages in their adult careers to keep their stress level down.

Some babies are already trying to smile (or is that gas?). They're waving their little arms as if to say, "Look at me! I've got lots of antics up my sleeve, and as soon as I get out of this little crib thing, I can't wait to try them!"

Yet other babies already look powerful. Their eyes and body language say, "Hey, world, I'm ready to take you on . . . and don't think I won't do it." These ones will emerge as the leaders (and yes, sometimes as the bullies).

And so on and so on.

If you don't believe me, check out a nursery for yourself for fun and do some guesstimating of your own.

Better yet, sneak a peek into your own living room at the critters living with you. Those kids of yours were born with a certain genetic makeup, with a particular personality or temperament. And they still carry that makeup, don't they?

Your 16-year-old son shot out of the womb as high-strung and still is that way. He's currently teaching himself electric guitar (yes, in your living room) and simultaneously doing his homework. But you don't worry, because he's always been a straight-A student.

Your 12-year-old daughter was the baby who seemed to lay back and take everything in, especially the actions of her big brother. But she thrived in playtimes with friends as the leveler of the group. When other little kids got into fights, she calmed everybody down. Now that she has a cell phone, she's currently texting her friends with the skill of a mad woodpecker and occasionally glances at her homework.

> **Sneak a peek into your own living room at the critters living with you.**

Your 9-year-old son slid right out of that birth canal, and that's exactly what he does through life—slide. Things were easy for him since his older brother and sister treated him like a pet and did everything for him. One little pout and big sis was there to the rescue. When you were about to be annoyed with him, he would beam his baby blues at you and smile, and your irritation would disappear—like right now, when you were about to chide him for littering chips and beef jerky remainders all over your newly vacuumed living room floor. And homework? He's forgotten he even had any.

How Much Is Genes?

If you have birthed your children, each most likely has some physical characteristic that looks like you. Your blue eyes, your dark hair, that prominent nose you hated as a teenager, your recessive-gene toes.

In this day of genetic engineering (certainly a debatable, contestable area of science), we've all heard stories about people who want to make sure their kids have very high intelligence from birth.

Let's face it. You have to credit that some of the things you become in life are part of your genetic makeup. For instance, how tall or short you are and the color of your hair, eyes, and skin. Whether you tend to be slender, like my lovely wife, or a bit on the pudgy side, like me. Or whether you tend to be like a manatee or a caged badger in personality. Some people tend to take any stress in stride; others come out swinging.

Genes do determine specific aspects of who we are. For example, if you have a child who has lower intelligence than average, it's not likely he'll become a professor. And medical science has proven that those born to alcoholic parents have certain predispositions to alcohol, and if they start using it themselves, they can quickly become addicted to it.

So basic built-in genes do provide certain givens in our lives. They may define how we look, unless we choose colored contacts, plastic surgery, or lipo, or get a sex change.

But I am a firm believer that genes do not have to define us.

Here's what I mean. Let's say your little Festus, at 3, looks exactly like his uncle Harold. He even acts like him sometimes—totally undisciplined. But just because Festus looks and acts a little like his renegade uncle, does that mean he's destined to become his uncle?

Think about the movie *Superman* for a moment. Clark Kent is raised by his adoptive parents and can barely remember his biological parents, except for brief flashes. He has no idea of his genetic makeup until it's revealed to him and he's called upon to use it. Instead of being bound by it, he uses it to change the courses of rivers and bend steel with his bare hands to help people.

You can be the Superman or Superwoman in your family by thinking things through and using the techniques in this book to curb your child's voracious appetite for attention and power.

Allow me to get on my high horse for a minute. As a practicing counseling psychologist, I became sick at heart by the labels that popped up to excuse all sorts of behaviors. "Well, Dr. Leman," a mom told me, "he can't help it. He's ADHD. That's why he doesn't have friends." We have tolerated all kinds of behaviors and issues as acceptable, merely because they have a label. We as a society no longer expect the best of people. Instead of accepting labels as excuses for unacceptable behaviors, why not work with the child to counteract those behaviors?

When I dug more deeply with that mom, I discovered that it wasn't merely the child's lack of attention that was causing the problems; it was that the boy ruled the roost and had never been taught to be kind to others. So at age 9, he was introduced to the concept of sharing, which he should have been shown as a baby, and saying kind words, which even toddlers learn. And part of his hyperactivity was due to the fact that he was desperately doing crazy things to get attention because he craved friends so badly. Within a year of working on these behaviors, we worked past the label that had been so easily slapped on him. His grades rose and he gained two good friends. Today that boy is the manager of three restaurants in a chain and well thought of by his staff.

Why are you allowing your child to be defined by labels?

We've all seen examples of people who have overcome challenging starts in life to become strong finishers. Take Jackie Joyner-Kersee, six-time Olympic medalist. She was born into a very poor family and had severe asthma, and she and her brother often ate bread-and-mayonnaise sandwiches, because that was the only thing they had to eat. But she had great determination, willpower, and parents who believed in her and told her to follow her dreams. After her Olympic career ended, Jackie continued to make a difference in the lives of children and teens in the inner city of Saint Louis and around the globe.

> **Why are you allowing your child to be defined by labels?**

Jackie Joyner-Kersee had a genetic makeup that was predisposed to asthma, yet she became an amazing athlete. She grew up in limiting circumstances but refused to let those limits or the labels of *black*, *poor*, or *asthmatic* define her. She powered on for the gold—and won.

And her parents, who had tremendous influence over her, were there all along the way, believing in her and cheering her on.

"I Know Each One of You Like I Know My Own Smell"

My favorite movie of all time is *The Three Amigos*. It was made way back in 1986 and only got two stars, but I love it. I could watch it over and over; it's slapstick comedy at its finest. But, as beauty is in the eye of the beholder, some beg to differ. My beloved wife, Mrs. Uppington, says, and I quote, "That's the most juvenile movie I've ever seen."

El Guapo, Spanish for "the handsome one," is anything but. This ugly, tough guy tells his men in a raspy voice, "I know each one of you like I know my own smell." I love that line so much that I even gave a talk on it once.

As a parent, I know each of my five kids like my own smell. And I hope that you, too, would know your kids that well—well enough to know that what works for one kid won't work for another. Part of being a parent is realizing that all kids are unique; you can't treat them the same. One of your kids reads people; the other reads books. One loves sports; one loves music. Offering to take both kids to a raucous county fair might backfire. The one who loves being with people will be in her heyday. The one who loves books will be thinking, *Uh, can we go home? I'm on page 112 of a great sci-fi thriller.*

> **All kids are unique; you can't treat them the same.**

Insisting the whole family goes to a local baseball game might thrill your sports lover. But the entire time, the classical music lover will be thinking, *Enough with the "Take Me Out to the Ball Game" song.*

Doing things as a family together is important. But sometimes it's a good thing to divvy up the kids and do specific things that they're genetically programmed to love. Take your book lover to a book fair and give her $20 to spend on a favorite. Accompany your music lover to a symphony concert. Let each child enjoy learning more about their talents and abilities, but also work to spread their horizons so they try new things, especially if they tend to be cautious. Realize that each child will act, react, and communicate differently.

Know each of your children like you know your own smell.

About Special Children

For those of you who have special needs children, you have special children indeed, and they are the salt of the earth. But are you letting the labels define those children and how you view them? Or what you allow them to do? Let me introduce you to some of my special friends and the unique contributions they're making to the world.

Little Jesse, age 7, has never met a stranger. He's loving toward everyone he meets. This year he ran with his friends in his community's first Little Friends marathon (like Special Olympics) to raise money for a new special needs center. There wasn't a dry eye on that marathon route as 11 special needs children ran together with joy, stopping every so often to hug each other or someone along the route.

Harold, age 19, is the friendliest bagger you've ever seen at his local grocery store. People who step into line looking harassed always get a friendly smile and a "You have a great day, now."

Andrea, age 18, works at a local animal shelter. No one is more patient or loving with the dogs that are brought in, or more careful about making sure their water is fresh and their food dishes are filled.

Don't ever let a diagnosis—whether Down syndrome, Tourette's syndrome, Asperger's syndrome, ADD/ADHD, or anything else—define your child. And don't let that diagnosis be an excuse for you as a parent to allow inappropriate behavior either. Neither one does your child any favor. But encouraging their talents and unique contributions not only rewards them with positive self-worth but allows them to contribute to more people's lives than you could ever imagine.

Especially for Adoptive Parents

Mei Mi was part of a group of seventh graders who were asked to draw a family tree for a history project at school. She was stumped and not quite sure what to do. That's because she was adopted at the age of 6 months from China and then brought to America, her new home. She didn't know who her birth parents were, so how could she do a family tree?

That night at dinner, she was unusually quiet. When her mom asked her what was wrong, she explained the project. "Mom, I don't have a family tree," she said.

Her mom smiled. "I've got just the thing."

And she handed her my book *My Adopted Child, There's No One Like You* from her bookshelf.

I know I wrote that book, but I really love it. In the book, Little Bear has to do a family tree assignment and is all down in the dumps because he's adopted. "I don't have a family tree," he tells Mama Bear.

Wise Mama Bear says, "Oh, but honey, you do have a family tree," and then she proceeds to tell Little Bear the story of what adoption is all about.

It was the inspiration Mei Mi needed to draft one of the best family tree projects her veteran teacher had ever seen!

Adoptive parents, you have been given a great gift—a child from God Almighty to love and care for. You may know some of the child's genetic background, but other parts of it may come as a surprise down the road, such as allergies or physical or mental predispositions.

Your child may have come from Russia and may have had an alcoholic mother. If so, a smart parent pays attention to that and will do research on the ramifications.

If your child comes from Asia, she may have specific foods she can tolerate and not tolerate. She may be prone to respiratory infections, especially if you live in a colder climate.

Do any research you can to find out about the background of your child and the issues (physical, emotional, and mental) your child may have faced while in his birth parents' home or in his orphanage or welfare institution. If your child was adopted after toddlerhood, he may have additional fears of abandonment or not being loved for who he is. He may seek attention because he never had it among the crowd at the orphanage and desperately craves it. He may ask over and over about what you're doing for the day, because he has a need to know—a result of the lack of control and loss of power he faced at the institution.

Being forewarned and aware of your child's particular needs is always wise. But do not allow any labels to be set upon that child. Yes, she will have genetic influences, but the day-to-day relationship you have with her is far more significant in impacting the direction she will go in life. The two basic psychological needs of all children are the same: the need for belonging and the need for unconditional acceptance.

If You See a Turtle on a Fence Post . . .

There's a wonderful old adage: "If you see a turtle on a fence post, you know he didn't get there by himself." That's because turtles are not genetically predisposed to fly or to climb up tall, vertical objects (though they show themselves to be tenacious about hefting themselves up on logs, even if it takes hours). No, somebody had to help him along so he could see a view of the world from up there.

In other words, no matter who we are, where we came from, and where we're going, all of us have key people who helped us get to where we are now. For me, it was first my mother, father, sister, and brother; then a feisty high school teacher who told me I could do something with my life; and then my wife. These were all the people who challenged me to make something of myself and believed that I could do it.

Everybody needs that kind of encouragement.

Are you helping your turtle get on that fence post?

Powerful Ideas That Work

Our daughter, Charlotte, is special indeed. A doctor told my wife that she should abort Charlotte when we discovered she had Down syndrome. But we believe that all God's children are special and that he had a purpose for her life.

Charlotte's now 15, and she's had a lot of challenges to overcome (us too). People haven't always been kind in how they've treated her, but she smiles and hugs everybody anyway. When she turned 14, we decided to get her a cell phone, since she was in a special program that meant she was away from our home for two hours each day after school. We didn't want her to get lonely. Her 11-year-old brother helped her program our numbers into her phone and added the numbers of her aunts, uncles, cousins, and grandparents.

The next week I got surprise phone calls from many relatives. Charlotte had routinely texted them each morning with a happy, encouraging message. They loved it!

After we read some of your blogs about not letting labels define your kids and also encouraging them to use their specific talents for the good of others, we got an idea. We asked our local church for people who were discouraged and hurting. With their approval, we programmed their numbers into Charlotte's phone.

The result was astounding. Our Down syndrome child now texts 22 hurting people once a day with an encouraging message. The words may not always be spelled right, but she shares her "happy," as she calls it, with others in a unique way. And we all get to share in the joyful messages sent back that make us all smile. Like the one that came in today from a woman in the final stages of cancer: "You are the one who continues to care about me every day, even when others have forgotten. You make my heart happy. God bless you, Charlotte."

Luke, North Carolina

Power Points

- All children are born with a unique personality.
- Genes provide certain givens but do not have to define us.
- Labels are limiting.

7

What Does Environment Have to Do with It?

*All children develop a screenplay on life—
and how they fit in—from 18 months on.*

I want you to imagine two scenarios with me.

Imagine that a kid named Andy is brought up in Meanview, Oklahoma. The town more than lives up to its name—everybody is mean. There's not a kind person anywhere. Then Andy's mean parents get a divorce. They create such a ruckus that even the mean judge orders that Andy can't live with either of his parents. So at 9 years old, he goes to live with his grandparents in Kindness, Kansas. And in Kindness, everybody is kind. There's not a mean person in the entire town except for this kid, who just moved in.

How do you think Andy is going to treat others in Kindness? In a kind way or a mean-spirited way? Obviously, he'll treat them in a mean-spirited way. Why? Because that's what he grew up with.

All the influences around him—Mom, Dad, and everybody else in town—were mean. So Andy fell in line and acted like them.

Now imagine that a kid named Rob grows up in Thieveryville, Illinois. In Thieveryville, everyone is a thief. At age 12, Rob loses his parents in a robbery attempt and moves to Honesttown, Wisconsin. What will Rob's behavior be when he moves to a new town, where everyone is honest? When he finds a gold watch in the restroom of a café, will he take it to the cashier and ask him to try to find the owner? Not on your life. He'll keep that object of value. Why? Because that action is consistent with the environment he grew up with and how Rob sees himself in relationship to other people.

Once a personality is formed, it's pretty difficult to change. The kid who is allowed to be powerful through the teenage years will become very resistant to change. Short of spiritual renewal—a coming to grips with who his Maker is and who he is—that prodigal is going to have a hard time changing his thoughts and behaviors.

It's a Small World After All

In the continuing tug-of-war in the nature/nurture debate, I believe we don't need an either-or answer. Both genes and environment have influence over our lives, and it is the combination of those two factors that contributes significantly to who we become.

But if I had to pick between the two as to which was the larger influencer, I would cast my vote for environment.

Think about your child's world for a moment. Most children have a very simple world—Mommy and/or Daddy, home, pets, and a few assorted relatives who come in and out of their lives. The title of the Disney ride applies: "It's a Small World." And it really is. All of those key influencers have a great deal to do with how that child grows up. That's why I always tell young parents, "When you're ready to have children, move as close to one set of grandparents as possible. If they're good people and not toxic, they'll be a wonderful influence on your child's life."

Many of us grew up in communities where an uncle, an aunt, or a neighbor didn't hesitate to correct a child's behavior if he or she was out of line. Contrast that to today in America, where if a teacher even touches a kid's hand, he could end up in litigation and out of a job. We've lost our sense of community and responsibility.

But for children to feel safe, loved, and as if they belong, they need both community and responsibility, because the people you choose to have around your children have a tremendous impact on them. And the words that come out of your mouth and the way you behave toward your children make all the difference in the world. That's why the old adage of "count to 10 and walk around the house before you say something you don't mean" was one of my mama's favorites (I'm sure she had to use it a lot with me), and it will assist you in a balanced approach to your child rearing.

Think of it this way. How would your parenting approach change if you realized that every word and every action of yours contribute to the way your child looks at life and her role in it?

Your Child's Screenplay

You've probably seen dozens of movies by now in your life. Even if you saw three on the same subject, they were most likely very different in how that subject was played out. Why is that? Because they were created by different people. Two people could have the very same experience but, because of their backgrounds and perspectives, have completely different views of that event.

The same is true of children. From age 18 months on, your children are busily developing their own screenplay on life—their view of looking at life that is unique to them.

It includes things such as:

- *Oh, I see, if I take my plate with all these green things (peas) on it and flip it over my head, my parents will think it's really funny.* (At least the first time. After 50 times, well . . .)
- *If I make a raspberry with my lips, adults turn their heads. Dad thinks it's hilarious, and Grandma gets annoyed. This is fun.*

And an entertaining, powerful kid is born. He knows he can make people laugh, provoking emotional responses by his actions.

Very early in life a child begins writing his own screenplay based on how his parents react to simple things. If the parents make the child the center of attention, the child thinks, *This is great. Not only my own screenplay, but I'm the star in the play—the main lead.* So your child begins to live out the worldview that says, "I'm the most important person of all. I only count when I control or dominate the scene."

You're not doing your kid any favors if you make him the center of the universe. Sure, you may think he's the cutest kid around, but if you treat him that way, I doubt others will think he's cute at all. In trying to be good parents, we often go overboard, providing our children with all the best opportunities, giving them things (even if we can't afford them and have to work a double shift to do so), and coddling them and protecting them from reality's consequences. Yes, we are to love and protect our kids, but if we overdo it, we create kids with a voracious appetite for power—children who think no one else matters but them. If you want an eerie portrayal of such kids, watch the movie *Charlie and the Chocolate Factory*.

For those children, the worldview of "I only count when I'm the center of the universe" becomes part of their psychological profile. It will influence how they think of themselves, how they view others,

> **You're not doing your kid any favors if you make him the center of the universe.**

and how they behave not only as children but as adults. Right now your child, no matter what age, is still developing that screenplay.

And his siblings and birth order have everything to do with it.

The Family Play

Sande and I used to enjoy—*endure* might be a better word—plays that our kids would put on for us when they were little. Holly, our firstborn, was always the star. Krissy, our secondborn, would get to introduce the star and hold up her hands adoringly as Holly came center stage in the Leman family room. And the baby of the family, Kevin II? He was lucky. He was always the dog.

Kids develop their screenplay by looking up. They're more influenced by who's ahead of them in birth order than who's behind them. That's why only children and firstborns in a family are always watching Mom and Dad to see how to respond to the world. Secondborns are eyeing the firstborn. And the thirdborn is keeping tabs on the secondborn and the firstborn.

Think of families you know who have two or more children. First, look at the firstborns. Get a picture in your mind of their qualities—how they look, how they dress, and their basic personality.

Then move to the secondborn child in that family and note those same things. If there's a thirdborn, again note the same things.

Notice the physical, emotional, and personality differences of those three cubs who came out of the family den.

Now think of the family you grew up in and do the same exercise. Doesn't history repeat itself?

Now think of your own kids and carry out the same exercise.

The firstborn and secondborn are as different as night and day, aren't they? Most likely, if you have a powerful child in the firstborn position in the family, there's a manatee or slug following—the kid who simply goes with the flow because he's chosen not to compete.

When a firstborn is flying high, being an exemplary role model, the secondborn takes a swift look and says to himself, *That role is filled. I'm going a different direction.* It's often the opposite direction.

That's why firstborns and secondborns in a family are usually vastly different. And the baby of the family finds a role all his own. Remember Kevin II, who was always the dog in the play? I remember once he made himself a sign that said "APPLAUSE" in big capital letters and hung it around his neck. You gotta give the boy credit. Even at his young age, he knew his role in the family, and it was very different from his sisters'. Today he's a very creative comedy writer for the funniest daytime TV program, and he's also won eight Emmys.

We're all actors in the play of life, and we tend to act within both our developed worldview and our birth order.

Firstborns: The Stars

My dad grew up in a poor Irish immigrant family of four brothers. He was number three. He used to say that the first sibling up in the morning was the best dressed, because they got their pick of the few clothes that they had.

And so it is with firstborns. Firstborns get first crack at everything. They're going to choose the path that seems right for them, and whatever path that is will vastly change the path of the child who directly follows them. If you're lucky enough to have a little manatee in the firstborn position of your family—in other words, a cooperative, delightful, helpful child—my best guess is that your secondborn is going to be more like a saber-toothed tiger.

The firstborn is the only one in the family play whose models in life are adults. That's because they're the first on the scene, and there's nobody else (at least for a while) on the family stage other than him and his parents. It's not that the middle **Firstborns get first crack at everything.** or youngest child doesn't see the two creatures called parents walking around the house, but there's a buffer between them—siblings.

Firstborns are held to a higher standard, because they're the first. The parental eagle eye is focused on them. They have to be the role model to the younger siblings. They're the most likely to be put upon to take care of their siblings. They're told to be kind to them and to share with them because their siblings are younger. And all the while, the firstborns are thinking, *This isn't fair. It's my candy, so why should I share with them?* And when firstborns grow up, the candy becomes things like computers, DVDs, even a car.

They also have a desire to know the details of a situation and are often uncomfortable without a schedule. They have a black-and-white view of right and wrong. They're the birth order who tends to feel the most stress and who tends to be involved in the most clubs and activities—president of the math club, working in the library on a volunteer basis, the football star.

Knowing these things about your firstborn, how would you respond to the following situations?

Scenario #1

Your son doesn't want to go to Grandma's birthday party. He has an offer to play with his buddies.

Wanna Fight Answer: "You're going. End of discussion." (And the word war ensues, with the slamming of doors and the stomping to follow.)

Balanced Answer: "Honey, I know you don't want to go to Grandma's house and you'd much rather play with your buddies. But it's Grandma's birthday, and we want to honor her on this day. I work five days a week and get two days off, just like you go to school five days and get two days off. That means there are things we'd like to do that we can't do. There are times in life you'll be asked to do things you don't want to do, like today. Trust me" (and laugh to break the tension) "there are times when the alarm goes off at 4:30 a.m. that I don't want to get up and take the train to the city. But I do it because I love you and your sister."

Scenario #2

Your daughter is tired of being the only one who takes the garbage out.

Wanna Fight Answer: "It's your job. Just do it."

Balanced Answer: "Let me ask you something. Do you really think your 3-year-old brother can wheel the garbage out? No, he's too little. You're a strong 12-year-old who can wheel that trash can down the driveway with no problem. I know it seems unfair, and I know you have a strong sense of what's fair and just, but I'm asking you to do it as your contribution to our family."

What's the difference between those types of answers? One provokes a fuss and a combative attitude; the other provides a teachable moment about life. When you're a parent, you're also a psychologist. Instead of your child getting attention the negative way—by fighting with you about things she thinks are unfair—direct her toward more positive thinking and goals.

Firstborns tend to be perfectionistic (after all, they were the star of the show that everybody was focused on before that sibling came along). Being careful and determined to do your best job is one thing. But the perfectionist is a powerful person who can't cope with life if it isn't perfect, and that's a dangerous proposition, because life is never perfect.

On the surface, a perfectionist may look like he has his act together. But then a teammate makes an error in a ball game and he throws a hissy fit. Or he does something wrong and he melts down. Or someone criticizes her and she wilts—or starts screaming about *all* of life being unfair (there's that black-and-white perspective popping up its head), when it's only one small thing she has been asked to do differently.

Firstborns can also be heavy-handed, rigidly insisting on the rules and trying to manage everything in their siblings' lives. When I originally wrote *The Birth Order Book*, I called it *Abel Had It Coming*. I thought it was a very clever title and it would catch readers' attention. And of course everybody knew about the infamous warring sibling duo, Cain and Abel, and how different they were. They were the perfect role models for my birth order theories.

The publisher said, "Uh, we can't call it that."

I replied, "But it's funny, and it's got a nice family flavor."

And the publisher said, "Well, you can't."

So I threw my own temper tantrum (note: I've grown since those days), folded my arms, and said, "Okay, then *you* name it."

They sat around their big oak table and came up with a provocative title: *The Birth Order Book*.

I can guarantee you those brainstormers were a bunch of firstborn children. But the title stuck. And I admit the book has done well. So maybe those firstborns are often right, after all.

What you can do

- Let your child see the difference between being a perfectionist and a pursuer of excellence. A perfectionist quits when things aren't perfect; he's defeated. A pursuer of excellence stays determined; he doesn't let failure deter him.
- Tell him often how much you appreciate him and what he does for his younger siblings.
- Give him extra privileges as the oldest in the family. Since he carries the heaviest weight of responsibility, he deserves it.

Middleborns: The Mediators

Middleborns like the highway of life to be smooth—no road bumps, no relational hassles. They're stuck in the middle between siblings who are often at war, so no wonder you find them hiding out in their room sometimes when they get tired of being the peacemakers. They're also the ones most likely not to be missed at the dinner table if the family is large, since they don't make waves and rarely talk in the group. With a star firstborn and a cute baby of the family, they don't shine upon first notice.

But don't let any appearances fool you. Middleborns, because of their role in the middle, usually navigate life with a sense of balance that calms everyone around them. They also become the best marriage partners—they're even-keeled and can see both sides of an issue, because they've been the frequent negotiator in their siblings' opposing views.

Krissy and Hannah, the second and third daughters in our family, are as steady as you could imagine. Krissy is one of the best moms I know to our grandkids, Conner and Adeline. Her approach to any quandary is balanced, and she looks for those teachable moments. Hannah has a passion for helping the poor and the vulnerable. She is able to see both sides of any argument and all facets of a program and put together a mutually workable solution for all.

> **Middleborns like the highway of life to be smooth—no road bumps, no relational hassles.**

The most important thing to remember about middle children is that they often don't feel needed or wanted by anybody because they feel squeezed between the crown prince or princess firstborn and Little Schnooky, who gets away with far too many things.

Knowing these things about your middleborn, how would you respond to the following situations?

SCENARIO #1

You notice your middleborn's eye roll at her older brother's bossiness.

Wanna Fight Answer: "Did you just roll your eyes at your brother? Young lady, that's not very nice. Go apologize now!"

Balanced Answer: "Wow, your brother's a little off the chart sometimes, isn't he? I've noticed that he sure does like to boss you around."

What your middleborn is now thinking: *Hey, how did Mom get inside my head?*

"I really appreciate your patience with him," you continue. "Even when he eggs you on, you don't fall for it. He's under a lot of stress. It makes me dizzy just looking at all those college brochures; I can't imagine how he feels. But I'm sorry he takes his frustration out on you. That's sure not fair, is it?"

Middleborn: *She gets it. What every day of my life is like. Keep talking, Mom!*

"Do you want to do something special this week, just you and me? And we'll leave bossy boy at home?"

Scenario #2

Your middleborn gets yelled at by your husband for something the baby of the family did.

Wanna Fight Answer: "Well, you're older. You should have known better and stopped her!"

Balanced Answer: "Your sister is quite good at manipulating others, isn't she? Even your dad sometimes."

Middleborn: *You got that right.*

"In fact, I noticed that he got on your case for what she did. I know you're often caught between your big brother and your little sister, and you seem to get the raw end of the deal. But I want you to know how much you matter to me and how important you are to our family. I don't know what we'd do without you. You're always so levelheaded. I wish I'd been more like you when I was your age."

Middleborn: *Wow. She wishes she were more like me?*

What you can do

- Mention frequently to your middle child how important she is to you and to the family.

100

- Win your middle child's cooperation.
- Set aside times where you can spend time just with your middle child.

Babies of the Family: Natural Entertainers

Babies of the family are seen as the family mascots, almost like pets, because they're the youngest. They're the "cute" ones who get away with murder. They're the entertainers who keep their parents hopping and are most likely to break the family rules—and not be punished for it. In fact, the older ones who "ought to know better" get blamed for their antics.

Babies will do anything for attention. They work hard at it, since they peer up the chain and see that intimidating firstborn flying high and getting all the awards.

> **Babies of the family are seen as the family mascots, almost like pets, because they're the youngest.**

Both older siblings also tend to order the baby around. He's the one most likely to be told, "Go and get me a Pepsi" when his siblings are watching TV and eating popcorn. And his siblings don't ask; they tell. But the baby of the family doesn't hold grudges. He simply likes to have fun.

Because the baby is the youngest, he's a master manipulator in getting his older siblings to do his chores by acting helpless. He also isn't crazy about books—unless they have a lot of pictures—but he loves people and can read them like books. He'll make a great salesman someday, at the top of his craft. That's because he's never met a stranger and has a delightful, winsome personality.

Knowing these things about your baby of the family, how would you respond to the following situations?

Scenario #1

You get a call from his teacher at school about his antics.

Wanna Fight Answer: "Young man, I talked to your teacher, and she told me what you did in class today. Stop it. Stop it right now! You ought to be ashamed of yourself!"

Balanced Answer: "One of the things I love about you is that you like to have fun, and you're always smiling. In fact, your teacher told me today that if they gave grades for having fun, you'd be the valedictorian of your school. When you and your brothers used to do plays, they thought they were the stars, because they gave themselves the talking parts. But you were the one who stole the show. That's because you're so good with people—you know how to make them laugh.

"Your teacher told me about some of the things you did in school today to get a laugh. Are you feeling uncomfortable in class? Are you hoping that people will like you? Pay attention to you? If so, you don't have to do what you did today. People will naturally be drawn to you—so much so that you could be a really good influence on them. The next time you're tempted to do your rendition of a wild turkey call in class, think about the fact that you don't have to make a fool of yourself to be noticed."

Scenario #2

She brings home her best-effort science paper, with a C.

Wanna Fight Answer: "I can't believe you got a C. Next time you have to work harder. I know you can do better if you'll try harder."

Balanced Answer: "You studied hard, didn't you? I couldn't be more proud of you for getting a C in a subject that's difficult. Yeah, your older brother is a brainiac, isn't he? Always has a book in his hand. But just because he gets better grades, does that make him a better person? Sometimes he takes himself too seriously; he's hard on himself.

"Whenever you're around, you add joy to our family. Remember the other night when you balanced a kernel of corn on the end of your nose, and then reached up with your tongue and snapped it? You looked like a frog. I was thinking of that yesterday when I was driving and nearly ran off the road laughing. I'm glad you're working your hardest at school. I expect your best shot. But I don't always expect As."

What you can do

- Make sure he pulls his share of the family load.
- Model a balance of fun and hard work.
- Teach long-range perspective and responsibility.

King or Queen of the Hill

When I was young, we played a game called King of the Hill. We found a pile of sand or dirt where a new home was being built, and as soon as the workers left for the day, the games could begin. The object was for you to be at the top of the hill and stay there. When others came to push you off the top, you'd try to push them down the hill.

Every kid in a family strives to be king or queen of the hill. They're looking for attention and they're craving power. And if they don't feel that they have some contribution to the family and some power over their life, they'll become powerful.

At times, you as the parent may think, *Why can't you be like your brother or sister?* There's a simple reason. Because your child is not that brother or sister. He's a completely different person. Expecting him to be like someone he isn't will only lead to frustration for both of you. Kids do enough comparisons on their own. They don't need further remarks from you.

They're too busy pushing their siblings off the hill.

Powerful Ideas That Work

One of my kids stole money out of my wallet this week, but nobody fessed up. I knew one of my three was lying and had a pretty good idea which one. I also knew forcing the issue wouldn't help her confess. So I followed your recommendation: B doesn't happen until A is completed. I decided we wouldn't go anywhere until we got to the bottom of it—not to Grandma's house for dinner like we'd planned, not to school, and not to any outside activities. Instead I told them, "I want each of you to go to your room, and I'm going to be in my room. All you have to do is write a note, sign it, and tell me what you did. Until I get that note, you all have to stay in your room."

Within the hour, my middle child couldn't take the stress. She decided to own up to it even though she hadn't done it, just to make peace in the family. But my firstborn was so guilt-ridden, she beat my middle child to it. She felt so bad for violating the family rule.

Your advice worked. We got to the bottom of the issue fast—without the usual yelling and accusations—and life could go on.

Kate, Pennsylvania

──────────── **Power Points** ────────────

- We all develop our own screenplay on life and act accordingly.
- Firstborns need perspective, appreciation, and privileges.
- Middleborns need to be understood, to feel important, and to have time set aside just for them.
- Babies need fun, work, and balance.

8

Raising Attila the Hun

Why parents unwittingly create powerful children . . . and what you can do about it.

"My Jackie would never do a thing like that," my spunky grandmother insisted.

Her defense of my older brother was vehement. Someone had accused him of throwing rocks at the goldfish in the eight-by-ten-foot pond in her backyard.

Imagine her shock when my honest brother owned up to it. "Yeah, I was trying to bomb those fish."

My grandma couldn't believe it. As an Irish woman, she was good about feeding us stories with a taste of blarney, and she'd thought someone was returning the favor. She was stunned when she found out the truth.

Isn't it true that you often give your own flesh and blood a natural pass on bad behavior?

Years ago, when I pointed out to Mrs. Uppington how obnoxious little Kevin was being at the time, she batted her eyelashes, smiled, and said, "Isn't he adorable?"

I said, "No, he's being a brat."

We often look at our own kids through rose-colored glasses. Every PTA parent believes in discipline . . . until it's their kid in the hot seat. Then they show up with attorney in hand and are concerned about the child's rights, instead of turning the behavior around.

It Starts with the Dream

Remember back when you were in love and dreaming of being married?

"Honey, I can't wait. Soon we're going to be in each other's arms every day. It'll be so wonderful. Then someday we'll have children. And they're certainly not going to be like your sister's kids."

Oh, the lies we tell ourselves. Now you're faced with a powerful child who makes your sister's kids pale in comparison.

How could all your dreams, wishes, and thoughts for that baby in your arms progress to daily power struggles with this power-driven kid who has badger-like qualities? What happened on the way from there to here? Weren't you the sweet, loving parents you thought you were before you said that sacred "I do"?

When your child first arrived in your home, you were overcome with the joy of being a parent. You counted that child's fingers and toes (don't tell me you didn't). And that 20-incher became a part of you and your family within seconds of seeing that miracle from God. You took the kid home and started the parenting journey with this person who was totally dependent on you for everything.

When you look back over the years, what went wrong? How could two normal people produce a kid who is so power-driven that there are times you don't even like to admit that he or she is your kid?

Let me put your mind at ease. You had everything to do with it.

You're the one who said to the kid, "I expect you to behave at the grocery store. If you don't, you're not going to get a treat."

What you unwittingly were saying is, "I know you're going to be an absolute brat at the grocery store, so I'm warning you right now. You better behave."

Now why would you expect something negative from your child? Why not expect something positive? In fact, why say anything at all? Is it a trek to the top of Mount Vesuvius or a simple trip to the grocery store? Why make it into a power struggle ahead of time?

Your kid's no dummy. Here's what she's thinking: *Oh, so Mom expects me to be good, huh? Well, I'll just show her a thing or two. I'm a great actress, and I know how to get attention. And if she gets embarrassed enough, she'll buy me off with a treat anyway. I'll get anything I want. So let's see, today I think I want . . .*

> **Why would you expect something negative from your child? Why not expect something positive?**

And yes, your child is that devious, but it's because she's been taught to be that way.

Truth is, you and your mate are the conduit for that power to have reached the level it has in your home today. You ignite the power rockets in your child when you fail to exercise your parental authority. If your child behaves one way at school, at Grandma's, and with her friends, and another way in your home, that's even more proof. You're trying too hard to be a good parent. And moms, here

I'm addressing you, because moms in general want their kids to be happy and strive to make their roads in life smooth. Dads tend to be more of the "suck it up" type, or they just shrug and go read the paper if the kid goes off (unless, of course, the dad comes from a damaged home background, and then he's likely to get combative).

If the powerful child is your secondborn, one of the things that set up that scenario was your firstborn. Most likely your firstborn is introspective and quiet and does life well. He's mellow and a nice kid to have around. In fact, he's so nice that it almost automatically sets up Attila the Hun in the next position. Your secondborn decides, *The good-kid part in the family play is taken, so I'll give them a run for their money.*

What You're Really Teaching

We parents unwittingly teach our kids the wrong things. A dad tells his son not to play at the edge of the woods because it's muddy. Ten minutes later, after listening to his son's continual whining about wanting to play there, the exhausted, annoyed dad relents. "Well, okay, but take your new tennis shoes off."

What's happened here?

First the parent tells the kid, "No, you're not going to play in the woods. It's too muddy."

Ten minutes later, that parent is worn down by the whining. Don't you think the kid knows it's going to work? He's got his dad figured out. Maybe company is over at the house, and the dad is embarrassed by his obnoxious kid and wants to get rid of him for a few minutes. Or he's had a long week at work, and he wants to put his feet up in that easy chair and channel surf. No matter the reason, that dad caves in.

The result? The kid not only gets to play where he wants, but his dad spots him out there in his new tennis shoes and doesn't do a thing. Two days later, when the kid complains that his shoes are all dirty and he can't wear them to school, what does that dad do?

"That's okay, Son. We'll go to Sports Authority after school tomorrow and pick up some new ones."

You don't need a PhD in psychology to figure this one out. The kid has learned that if he whines and persists, Dad will give in. And he'll not only get exactly what he wants, but more—those new shoes.

Pop quiz time. Who created that powerful child? And how did that child get powerful in such a short period of time?

Answer: the parent, who vacillated and wasn't consistent. He said no but then changed his mind to yes. Through trial and error, that child learned that if he continued an unwanted behavior long enough, he'd accomplish his goal of getting what he wanted—new shoes. When a powerful child's actions are successful, that child gains power for the next go-round.

In other words, we parents get what we ask for.

If you have a child who's bent in the direction of being powerful, you need to (1) be aware that the child is working you, and (2) be careful how that child works you.

If you have a powerful child, you're the one who has taught him to be that way.

The good news is that if your child has learned to be that way, he can unlearn it.

> **Pop quiz time. Who created that powerful child?**

Powerful or Normal?

There's one thing I want to caution you about. Parents read a lot of things into their child's behaviors. They take those behaviors personally when, in fact, what the child is doing is normal for his age and stage. For example, your 16-month-old is inching along your built-in bookshelf and pulls a book off of it. Or your 18-month-old has learned that he can get on his tippy toes, grab a car from his big brother's collection, and make it crash onto the floor.

What's your first reaction? "No, no, don't do that. We have to be careful with books." Or "Those are your brother's cars. Don't touch those."

But the kid continues to do it. Why? He's exhibiting developmentally appropriate behavior. Kids ages 16 to 18 months old love cause and effect. It wouldn't make any difference to them if the things they were dropping were antique goblets with a value of $200 apiece. They'd enjoy dropping them on the floor and hearing the shattering of the glass. It's fun. It's exciting to see what happens when you drop something. It's a new experience, filled with all sorts of wonderful sights and sounds. A truly joyful experience.

So when you tell a child that age, "Don't do that!" you know what he's thinking?

What on earth is wrong with my parents? I'm only doing what I'm supposed to do at this age.

But 99 percent of parents will read into that behavior and think their child is being willfully disobedient, and they will overreact. They'll think, *He's defying my authority.* Whereas the kid isn't doing anything like that—he's simply engaging in normal behavior for his age.

When your teenage son turns a shoulder to you and stares out the car window after school, you have to remember that he's processing what happened during the school day. He may not be ready to talk yet. If you provoke him to say something, the result won't be pretty.

As soon as you overreact to something simple, you begin to create a powerful child because you are being overly powerful in that situation.

In the above example, you should have just picked up the tyke and removed him from the scene. Even better, remove breakable things from shelves the kid can reach. It would certainly be less stressful for everyone.

And why not wait awhile for that teenager to talk? Silence really is golden. Later, bake some chocolate chip cookies (for those of you who aren't domestic, the tube from the grocery store will do) or make some popcorn, and watch the he-bear come out of his cave and start sniffing around. Food's wonderful to get teenagers talking. If you're patient, you'll find out a lot about his day—far more than if you pester him for information and he glues his mouth shut.

Don't confuse normal behavior with power. It doesn't become power until you choose to overreact.

A Surprising Power Source

Where does your powerful child get his power from? What's the power source?

Do you have a solar-powered son or daughter? Alkaline-battery-powered? Or could it be parent-powered?

When I ask parents in a seminar how many of them have a powerful child at home, nearly 95 percent raise their hands. There's no doubt in their minds. The other 5 percent are lying. Every family has a powerful child.

Then I ask, "How many of you would admit that one of the parents in the home—either you or your spouse, if you're married—is a powerful person?"

Hands drop and smiles falter.

Reality sets in.

Kids learn their power from somewhere.

Power can come from a lot of sources, but it starts with you, parent. You are the conduit that makes it easy for your child to become more power-driven. Now you're in the position of being a member of a bomb squad, called in to defuse a bomb. One wrong move, and *kaboom!* There will be another explosion—a power tantrum, a meltdown, an embarrassing situation in front of your neighbors or your boss at work. Our job in this book is to figure out how to safely defuse that child before the bomb goes off, and that means going back in their history to figure out how they got this powerful behavior in the first place.

Let's say a 4-year-old is sitting in his chair and refuses to eat. He arches his back, pitches a fit, then slides out of his chair to the floor, crying. Some parents would strong-arm the kid. "Get back in your chair right now and eat your dinner!" That's the authoritarian parent, with the need for order ("We have dinner at X time, and you'd better eat it or else") and power ("I'm the parent, and I'm in charge here"). The permissive parent will let them go and then, half an hour later, feel guilty that the kid hasn't eaten. ("Oh no, little Buford will starve to death. I'll just give him a little snack.") So that parent goes out of their way to make a special snack that Buford will love.

Kids learn their power from somewhere.

Either way, little Buford wins. He's out of that chair and about his business. Who cares if Dad yells? Buford doesn't want that old dinner anyway. He wants to play. And if he has to put up with a little yelling to get what he wants, it's like water off a duck's back. He knows Mom will feel bad and make his favorite snack later anyway.

But what if, instead, the scene went like this:

"Buford, it looks like you don't want to eat dinner right now. If you're not hungry, that's okay. But you will sit here quietly while we eat our dinner, because we're a family and we eat dinner together."

So Buford's little plan of getting out of the chair and playing is foiled by the parent's calm, reasoned statement. Sure, Buford might kick up a fuss the first few times Mom or Dad does this—after all, kids are entrepreneurial. They'll try different things until they hit on something that works. But Mom simply says calmly, "In this family we eat dinner around the table. Notice that Dad is sitting in his chair, and Big Sister is sitting in hers, and I'm sitting in mine. And we all eat dinner together." Powerful kids will sometimes refuse to eat. But if you call and ask your pediatrician, "If a child misses a meal, will he die?" the answer is no. But the child will learn a very important lesson about you, the parent, not backing down.

So later, little Buford is hungry. He asks for his favorite snack. What does Mom do? "Sure, I'd be happy to make that for you, if you're still hungry after you eat your dinner." So the kid climbs back in his chair and is served the same plate he refused to eat at dinner. Mom doesn't back down about that snack until after the dinner is completely finished. By then, the kid isn't hungry anymore.

Now, what did that kid learn? *I might as well have dinner with the folks and spend time with them, since I'll have to eat that same dinner sometime anyway.*

See how it works?

When you act as an authoritarian or permissive parent, chaos always follows in the wake of any actions. Here's why:

Children
Have
Arsenals
Of
Strategies

So be a smart parent. Don't fall for the strategies. Your goal is to teach your child how to deal with life without kicking off the power game, for when you wield power, all you're asking for is a kid to be powerful in return. And that's a losing proposition for both of you.

Who Is Your Powerful Kid?

As I've said earlier, power comes in different packages.

Your powerful kid might be your firstborn, who acts very timid in every new situation because he doesn't know what's expected of him.

Think of it this way. If you're walking into a lake in summertime and you've never been there before, would you jump in with both feet? No, you'd probably stutter-step to see where the lake bottom drops off, ask how deep it is, and so on. But once you know the details, if you're a swimmer you'll jump right in.

Most powerful people are cautious when they don't know what the rules or expectations are, but when they do, watch out—they'll run right over you! However, until they're sure, they'll test the water, because they have a need to be right. They might appear to be thick-skinned, but they're not. They actually lack confidence; they don't want to make fools of themselves.

Your powerful kid might be your middleborn, who has decided that she only counts in life if she wins or dominates or controls. She might also procrastinate, not moving forward until she's certain she'll get the result she needs.

Your powerful kid might be your baby of the family, who doesn't understand the word *consequence* because he's never been faced with one. He's always gotten away with everything because he was the littlest and cute.

Tag, You're It!

I want to ask you a very important question. Do you find yourself in the same argument with your son or daughter every day? Be honest. If you are, you'll answer, "Yes." How does this tag-team event work? Let me talk it through with you.

Scenario #1

You start off by reminding your son that the clock is ticking, and he's going to be late for school.

What does he say?

"Oh, I didn't hear my alarm." Or "I'm too tired to get up." Or "I don't want to go to school today." It's always some excuse.

What do you do next?

You tell him to get his butt out of bed now, because the bus is on its way.

What happens next?

He ignores you and rolls over. Five minutes later, you go to his room and start yelling at him to get out of bed. He finally does. But by then, the bus is gone and you have to drive him to school.

So what did you just do? Ratchet up your heart rate and stress, and then mess with your schedule. And what did he get? What he wanted—a few extra minutes in the sack plus your attention, even if it was negative.

Fighting is an act of cooperation; it takes two to do battle. So stop inciting the battle from your end. Do the following—without any warnings or threats. Don't even tell the kid you've launched your plan. Keep the secret to yourself.

Scenario #1 Replayed

When the alarm goes off and the kid ignores it, you don't do *anything*. No reminders. No visits to his room. No tantalizing breakfast smells to encourage him to get up. Get out a book, have some coffee, and wait out the rest of the scene. Smile when you see the school bus stop for a minute and then whiz away.

Fifteen minutes later, your son comes stumbling down the stairs, bleary-eyed and rumpled. "Mom, it's 8:50!" he says in a grumpy tone.

"Oh?" you respond calmly.

"Why didn't you get me up? Now I'm going to be late!"

"I guess you're going to be late," you say and return to your book.

"Mom!" he says, powering up, "I've got a test at 9:00."

"I guess you'll have to explain why you're late." Back to your book, with your feet up.

"We gotta go now! You've gotta drive me!" By now your son has grabbed his backpack and a banana for breakfast.

"I'm almost finished. I'll be with you in a couple minutes," you say. And you continue to read.

Now your son stops cold, looking completely confused. It gets better. He insists you write him a note. "Say I was at the doctor's or something, so I won't get marked late."

You shake your head. "Nope. You'll need to explain to the office why you were late."

He stares at you in shock. "You aren't serious!"

You smile. "I'm completely serious," you say.

Finally you drop him off at the front door of the school. "Have a good day, and I'll see you this evening."

And off you drive. You go through the Starbucks drive-through, reward yourself for your follow-through with a tall chai latte, and laugh yourself silly for five minutes.

Do you think that after today, your kid might get up by himself? You bet.

Scenario #2

Jared, a third grader, is sitting at the breakfast table still in his pajamas. He's been stirring his Cheerios for exactly seven minutes. It's time to leave for school. He always dawdles when you need to get out the door, and it's driving you crazy. (Remember that procrastinating is a power behavior.)

What would you usually do?

"Jared, hurry up. You've got to get changed now or you'll be late for school. We're leaving in two minutes!"

When he continues to dawdle, you hustle him to his room like a clucking hen and "help" him (because of course he's helpless and can't get dressed by himself).

By the time you get out the door, you're so stressed and sweaty you feel like you need a second shower.

But what if you did the following instead?

Scenario #2 Replayed

Jared is sitting in his pajamas at the breakfast table, stirring his Cheerios.

You eye the clock—8:25.

You've been ready for this moment ever since 6:30, when you got up with that gleam in your eye. You packed his lunch, his backpack, a set of clean underwear, jeans, a shirt, and his tennis shoes and stashed them in the car.

"Jared, you have two minutes before you have to meet me in the car."

He continues stirring his Cheerios and doesn't acknowledge you.

Two minutes later, you pick up your purse and car keys and open the door to the garage. "Time to go."

Jared looks up, startled. "But Mom, I'm not even dressed yet."

"Your backpack and clothes are already in the car."

Stunned, the little sheep follows you to the car and gets in. When you're a block away from school, he exclaims, "I'm still in my pajamas! I can't go to school like this!"

"Well," you say calmly, "I'm going to pull over in this parking lot, and you'll have exactly one minute to change. If you don't, I guess you'll be wearing your pajamas to school today."

You pull over in the spot you figured out hours ago, count exactly 60 seconds, and grin all over inside as your son scrambles as fast as he can to get dressed (he really can do it when he wants to).

Miracle of miracles, when you arrive at school a couple minutes later, the kid is dressed, but he looks a little shell-shocked.

So much the better.

You drive away, smiling, strategizing how you can now move to the next stages: having him get dressed at home and pack his own backpack. But you're on your way, because you've realized something important: you can't back down with this kid—ever—and hope to accomplish anything. You're going to have to stick to your guns.

Scenario #3

Little Emily grabs your skirt and hides her face behind your thigh anytime she meets someone. What do you normally do?

"Emily, what do you say, honey? Can you say hello to Mrs. Jacobs?"

The kid doesn't come out.

With a little laugh to Mrs. Jacobs, you say, "Oh, she's a little shy today."

You make excuses for the kid. The adult goes away, and Emily comes out. What has Emily learned? *Mom will run interference for me. That's kinda fun. Especially since I like the soft material of her skirt anyway. It's kinda like my blankie.*

Emily will go on controlling your home and will up her power every time you let her off the hook.

Scenario #3 Replayed

Little Emily grabs your skirt and hides her face behind your thigh when you go to visit Mrs. Jacobs. You take her gently by the hand and move her in front of you, clasping both your hands on her shoulders.

"Mrs. Jacobs, this is my daughter, Emily," you say.

The kid tries to wrestle out of your hands and go behind your skirt.

You calmly keep your hands on her shoulders, holding her in front of you, and go on talking to Mrs. Jacobs.

If she wrestles out of your control, you calmly draw her back in front of you and proceed talking. You give Mrs. Jacobs a wink, and if she has any smarts, she'll get that you are trying to teach your daughter a valuable lesson and play along.

"Mrs. Jacobs," you say, "I know you have a very special collection of dolls from all around the world. I'd love it if you'd be willing to show it to Emily and me someday. Emily really loves dolls."

Now you've piqued your child's interest, and she's forgotten that she's trapped in front of you.

"You have dolls?" she asks. "What do they look like?"

Without realizing it, she stops struggling and takes a step away from you and toward Mrs. Jacobs.

You smile. You are one smart parent.

Instead of allowing your powerful child to ramp up her behavior, you've shown her a benefit of not continuing that behavior. And she fell for it, just like you knew she would.

Later you can thank Mrs. Jacobs for playing along.

Now you try it.

Scenario #4

Your son refuses to bathe, and he's getting rather aromatic. You don't want anyone at school—or anywhere else—to get a whiff and send out the dirt police to your house.

Scenario #4 Replayed (4- or 5-Year-Old)

What would you do? Brainstorm . . .

Scenario #4 Replayed (Teenager)

What would you do? Brainstorm . . .

Now, I'll tell you what I'd do. I'd take both powerful buzzards by the beak, because one of the basic tenets in life is cleanliness. It's especially important that boys get this concept, because otherwise they'd wear the same underwear for a week, then turn it inside out and wear it another week. They wouldn't even think a thing about it—unless, of course, they're powerful kids who know how much that bothers you, keen-nosed Mom, and then they'll go out of their way to protest any bath or clean clothing as a matter of principle.

If the 4- or 5-year-old won't bathe himself, then bathe him like he's never been bathed before. Wash his face so thoroughly that he'll say, "Okay, okay, I'll wash it." Yes, you stopped bathing him when he was a toddler for the sake of privacy, but all bets are off now.

To make the bath more palatable, throw in a few things to play with. I know one girl who hated baths until her grandma started adding plastic spoons, butter tubs, and other kitchen castoffs to the water. Then she'd play in there for hours.

For the teenager, this simple principle applies: B doesn't happen until A is completed. That means if he walks by you on the way out the door to an activity that you're driving him to and your sniffer recoils, you simply say, "I can see you're not ready to go. I can tell by your breath and your BO that you're not prepared to leave the house." He'll look at you in shock; he'll argue about being late. But B doesn't happen until A is completed.

You say calmly, "When you're ready, I'll be more than happy to drive you there."

Yes, that teenager might test you to make sure you're serious. "Okay, I'll take a shower as soon as I'm home."

B doesn't happen until A is completed.

But you hold firm until your teenager gets the fact that you're not moving until your sniffer is satisfied.

I guarantee he'll stomp off to make a point. He might even do a little yelling. He'll certainly argue.

But hold firm. If you don't, you won't accomplish anything.

When he comes back, do another sniff test. If you're satisfied, out the door you go. If not, you can say, "That was a little too quick. Try again."

You can bet the next time he'll be prepared and smellin' good! I guess the old saying is true: "Nobody messes with Mama." But I'd have to add, "Unless Mama allows herself to be messed with in the first place."

It's always tough to take off those rose-colored glasses and scrutinize your kid. But doing so is a favor not only to your kid, yourself, and your family but also to the world that child will live in as a grown-up someday. The truth may pinch for a bit, but remember what I said earlier: when your child starts flailing wildly at the air like that hooked fish that doesn't want to be hooked, you know you're right where you should be to transform those power surges into positive urges.

Powerful Ideas That Work

I was sick of the every-morning fights with my daughter over what she wore to school. Same old, same old. She'd insist on wearing tight shirts and short skirts; I'd insist on her not wearing them. We always got into a big fuss and ended up mad at each other. Shopping together was impossible.

Right before she started her freshman year of high school, I read *Have a New Teenager by Friday* and got some great ideas. I handed her money to spend on her school clothes, dropped her off at the mall with friends, and picked her up four hours later. I didn't say a word about her purchases; I didn't even ask to view them.

Her first day of school, she went out the door dressed in something I'd never want her to wear, but I kept my mouth shut. What she'd forgotten in her excitement about picking clothes out for herself was that this new school had a dress code. An hour later I got a call from the school. They asked me to pick my daughter up because she was inappropriately dressed, and they kept her in the principal's office until I could get there.

I didn't say a word. Just picked her up and drove her home to change. I didn't tell her what to wear, but she came back to the car wearing last year's jeans and the polo shirt I'd made her buy.

That day, what you call "reality discipline" set in. I didn't have to say anything. Being embarrassed at school did it all.

Every day after that, she was appropriately dressed to school code. Her wardrobe was limited all year—I'd already given her all the money we'd set aside for clothes and said there wouldn't be any more until the next year. But she learned a valuable lesson.

Soon she'll be starting her sophomore year. "Mom," she said the other day, "would you mind going shopping with me this year?" She even offered to save enough money to buy us lunch. Now we're talking. Your "reality discipline" theory works in the real world. It certainly worked in my world.

Francine, Minnesota

Power Points

- Recognize the difference between normal, age-appropriate behavior and powerful behavior.
- Don't set your kid up to misbehave.
- Strategize how to defuse the power in your everyday power struggles.

9

Why Kids Misbehave

*Don't let those cherublike faces fool
you. Your smart kids have goals.*

One of my goals in life is to make any kind of education informative and entertaining. That's why, when I was teaching at the University of Arizona, I made sure my classes were practical and hands-on in nature, and there was takeaway. Anyone who has read a Leman book knows you're not going to find a big chunk of high-and-mighty-sounding psychological research. Instead, you'll find informative, entertaining, practical material to help with real life. But there are a few people and ideas you need to know about because they directly impact you and your child.

Psychiatrist Alfred Adler is one. He believed that behavior had a purpose—he was the first to talk about that concept—and was instrumental in my thinking as I developed my own psychological theories on people, relationships, and life. Alfred Adler was at one time a colleague of Sigmund Freud's in Vienna, Austria. But a public debate once uncovered that the two colleagues saw life completely different.

If they were both alive and debating each other today, and they were asked why they thought people smoked, here's what they'd say:

Siggy: "You smoke cigarettes today because you were fixated on the oral stage of development at your mother's breast."

Alfie: "You smoke because you're stupid."

I like old Alfie. He was very practical. But if you've ever read Alfred Adler, it can be pretty heavy reading. It's a bit like trying to read *The Merck Manual* for fun on a Saturday night or picking up James Michener's *Hawaii* for a quick read. The guy was brilliant, but he used too many big words for me.

So along came Dr. Rudolf Dreikurs, a well-known and respected educator and a student of Alfred Adler's in the 1930s. He, too, believed that all behavior had a purpose, so he took a lot of Adler's academic-sounding materials and, for lack of a better term, westernized them into four goals of misbehavior so guys like me could understand them. The four goals, in order, were attention, power, revenge, and display of inadequacy. His book *Children: The Challenge* is a wonderful little book that's worthwhile reading for anyone who's interested in Adlerian theory applied to child rearing.

In all my years as a practicing psychologist, I've seen thousands of children. Less than 1 percent of them have passed the first two levels and moved on to revenge or display of inadequacy. Ninety-nine percent of them are at the attention and power levels. That's why, for the purposes of this book, I've chosen to address those two basic stages of misbehavior: (1) attention and (2) power.

Also, in the scope of my private practice, I dealt with generally "normal" people—within normal limits of behavior—and didn't deal with severely disturbed people (those beyond stage two). However, for your overall understanding of the goals of misbehavior, I'll do a quick pass over all four of them. Following Dreikurs, other people—notably Don Dinkmeyer and Gary McKay (a classmate of mine at the University of Arizona grad school)—have further refined Adler's theories and helped thousands of people, both parents and professionals, to understand the nature of misbehavior in children and what to do about it.

The most important thing for parents to know is that if a child doesn't receive satisfactory results in his striving for attention (the first stage), he then moves to power (the second stage), and so on. Remember what we discovered about behavior? It's purposive—it serves a purpose.

Attention: Stage One

Some kids live for being the center of attention, and they'll do almost anything to be noticed—which means everything from arguing constantly with you (even negative attention is attention) to being the clown at school or at home. They don't care what it takes to get attention, as long as they get it. These are the kids others can view as rude, annoying, and, at times, unacceptable. They might temporarily stop their attention-getting behavior when they are given attention, but that doesn't last long. In order to gain more attention, they often begin a new annoying behavior.

A child who is an attention-getter is mildly discouraged. He feels as if his opinions don't count, so he has to work hard to get any notice for himself. His life mantra is, *I only count when others pay*

His life mantra is, *I only count when others pay attention to me.*

attention to me. Oftentimes that child is dealing with the high expectations of a parent who pushes him to excel or talks about how bright a sibling is. The child feels like he can never measure up to such a high expectation, and he worries about it. So he works hard at entertaining or getting attention other ways.

How do you deal with an attention-getting child? We'll talk in depth about this later in the book, but here are a couple pointers for now. First, you ignore him when he *demands* your attention. You simply turn your back and walk away. But then you surprise him by giving him attention in unexpected ways—for positive behavior. You won't have to wait long—that kid of yours is smart. He'll soon be doing loops to get your attention in a positive way.

Kids start by seeking attention, but if they don't get attention, they move to the next level.

Power: Stage Two

Powerful kids simply want their way. They are willing to do whatever it takes to be in charge and stay in charge. Their life mantra is, *I only count when I'm dominant—when I can get others to do whatever I want them to, and when I can do whatever I want to.* They are the kids who disobey, are uncooperative, talk back, and don't show respect for others. They're the kinds of kids who continually challenge you, provoke you, and make you want to lash back with "So you don't want to do it? Well then, I'll make you do it. How dare you! You can't get away with that!"

If a child's needs for basic attention are not met in a positive way, and the parental expectations are not lowered to a realistic level for her abilities and talents, she ramps up to the next stage: power. She's thinking, *I have skills, and I'll show you who's boss. I'm going to control all the shots. So if good grades are all that's important to you, I can take care of that.* This child who was voraciously reading four books a week at home suddenly isn't doing as well at school. Parents begin to see slipping grades.

My advice? Parent, back off. If your child is devouring that many books, she's a natural learner. Communicate privately with the school faculty that you have faith in them. Then let the school take your buzzard by the beak and work with her in upping her accountability and responsibility in getting her homework done. If she's an athlete, she'll have some additional motivation: if she doesn't pull good enough grades, she won't be eligible to play. That's much better than you hovering over the kid, having the same argument—complete with tears, yelling, and slammed doors—that you have every night when you encourage her to do her homework.

> She's thinking, *I have skills, and I'll show you who's boss. I'm going to control all the shots.*

You be the adult. Choose to withdraw from the conflict. Put the ball in the court where it belongs, and don't go pick it up from the other side. If you put yourself on equal footing with your child, not as an almighty dictator but as a human being (even though you play different roles in the family), your child will no longer need to fight. It takes two to tango. You'll be amazed what happens as you and your child learn together to redirect all that negative energy (from both of you!) into constructive activities and a growing relationship.

Revenge: Stage Three

If a child's needs for attention and power are not met in a positive way, he moves to the next stage: revenge. If your child is at this stage, he needs more assistance than the scope of this book can give. These are the kids you read about in the paper. They're the ones who strike out against society and will likely spend time in prison. Their thinking is, *I've been so hurt by life that I have a right to hurt others.* Even when the others they hurt might be innocent individuals.

We've all read accounts of people in the newspaper or seen stories on television of those who've felt hurt by life and struck out at others in horrific ways. The shooting sprees at Sandy Hook Elementary School and Columbine High School are only two of the tragic examples that have left a number of children and teachers dead and many others injured. After their murderous rampage, the gunmen turned their guns on themselves.

> **Their thinking is, *I've been so hurt by life that I have a right to hurt others.***

In many cases, suicide is revenge. After all, you send a message when you kill yourself. It's the biggest spit in somebody's soup that you can give. *Take that,* you're saying. *I've been so hurt by life and by you that I'm going to fix this mess myself.* Suicide is their final act of revenge and gains the attention and power they seek by making the headlines. When people leave behind a suicide note, the words are always some rendition of "Take that."

Those kids who lash out in revenge—to get even—are compensating for real or imagined hurts. The revenge can be either physical or psychological. For example, bullies often use revenge to excuse their shoving, pushing, and teasing.

Many kids in the revenge stage have developed a life view that the world is not safe. As a result, they've never felt safe or secure, and they can't trust anyone. Their response when feeling hurt in any way is to strike back ("I'll show you . . ."), either by becoming juvenile delinquents or by taking their own lives since they can't measure up in their minds.

What's really sad is that these kids in the revenge stage started by seeking attention, which they didn't get. They then moved on to power, which didn't work either.

Revenge can also take a passive form, like the kid who won't say anything combative to people's faces, but behind their backs—watch out. How else do you explain people who sit on a freeway with a gun and pick off total strangers?

Most adults, when faced with a revengeful child, are at first hurt and shocked. *How can she do this to me?* they think. Then they get angry and try to get even, "punishing" the child. All that process does is increase the child's drive to seek revenge. There's no winning on either side of that battle.

What can a parent do? Get professional help right now. Don't wait. Try to maintain order with a minimum of rules (most of the revengeful kids have no respect for punishment or the punisher anyway), and take time to understand and build a bridge of trust with that child. No, change won't be instant, but nothing good in life ever is.

Display of Inadequacy: Stage Four

Some psychologists call this *assumed disability*. These are the kids who've given up on life. *I can't do anything right, so I won't even try at all*, they think. They decide to hide out rather than engage.

I once met a homeless man who lived under a bridge, and I discovered that he'd once been a brilliant engineer. Another homeless man, who was selling newspapers on a street corner in Tucson (the local paper allows homeless people to sell papers to make some money), worked on a book of crossword puzzles in between sales. Anyone who does crossword puzzles loves words and is a voracious reader. That means the man wasn't too low in brains. But something happened in that guy's life that was so devastating he gave up. So he sells papers, hoping someone will be generous.

People in stage four may be extremely brilliant and skilled in their fields, like the engineer under the bridge. Yet they feel that, no matter how well they do in that chosen field, they're never quite good enough. Life has so beaten them down that they don't care anymore. They've gone past the revenge stage to giving up on themselves, giving up on life. They're passive, never improving in any areas, because they feel it's useless to try.

Many grew up with a critical parent who was "shoulding" on them at every turn and telling them they could never measure up. If they had siblings, they heard frequently, "Why can't you be like your brother?" To avoid that failure, they simply gave up. They appeared to be discouraged and helpless. They didn't try anything, because trying could mean failing. They lived in the shadows, hoping others would forget about them and not hold them responsible for anything.

These are the people who, when they grow up, don't need any critics. They become the critical parent of themselves. Every time they do something, they remind themselves, *It's not good enough. You're not good enough.*

Let's say someone is an accomplished artist, and everyone is talking about how talented she is in watercolors and oils. But she can't hear or process what people are saying because that critical voice inside is screaming, *It isn't good enough. It'll never be good enough*. Or someone could be a successful businessman and make good money, but inside he's telling himself, *If those people only knew how that project should look, they wouldn't give me a dime for it.*

> **That critical voice inside is screaming, *It isn't good enough. It'll never be good enough.***

This behavior is self-defeating. In the animal world, it would be like the dog that cowers and hits the floor the instant it meets people. The logic is, *I'm going to get beat up in this situation, so I might as well put myself on the floor*. That's what stage four people do. They lay down before anybody can have a chance to knock them down.

Parents who are dealing with a stage four child feel hopeless and discouraged. They often simply give up, believing that change in their family life is impossible. That's not true, but it will take a lot of assistance from a professional who can work with not only the child but the parents as well.

The first way parents of these children can help is by encouraging any positive effort—even the slightest effort, such as picking a jacket up off the floor. They can also be overheard in "good gossip" with a friend on the phone, saying, "You know, Jimmy is amazingly good at technology. The other day, when I was stuck on a computer issue, he . . ." Children have excellent hearing; you can bet that Jimmy will hear your words.

Parents should also never give up, never fall into the "poor kid" or "poor me" trap, and *never criticize*. Patience and love, along with professional counseling for the entire family, will slowly win.

The goals of misbehavior are the reason some parents try all kinds of techniques to handle the same behavior problems over and over and get little or no results. As soon as parents find a way to stop one misbehavior, another behavior problem surfaces. It may look different on the outside, but it's based on the same goal of misbehavior. That's because the child still has the same underlying belief about himself. His view of who he is and what his role in the world is haven't changed.

For example, if a child thinks she only counts when she's getting attention or when others notice her, she'll continue to seek attention.

If he thinks he only counts when he's the guy in control—because then nobody can boss him around—he'll ramp up the power play.

Kids only misbehave when they have a reason—and their behavior works.

That's a truth you can count on.

Powerful Ideas That Work

My son, Kent, was 3 when we adopted his sister, Tricia. A short while after his sister arrived home, I caught Kent biting her on the arm. I was shocked and punished him for it.

Kent had been potty-trained for over a year, but he started wetting his pants. And he kept biting his sister or pinching her when I wasn't looking. Finally, I had to lock him in his room when she was taking a nap because I couldn't trust him.

I read a bunch of books and talked to a lot of parents over the next six months. I tried their advice, but nothing worked. He was still biting, pinching, and wetting his pants. And when he was 4, he told me he hated his sister.

The lightbulb went on when I read your *Birth Order Book*. Kent was jealous of his sister, yes. (I'd figured that much out. After all, I am a college graduate.) But he was also scared of being replaced by his sister. He wanted my attention—however he could get it.

That was clear. As a firstborn, he didn't like change and needed to know the ropes.

So when I found him trying his sister's diapers on, I got an idea. I leaned down and whispered in his ear, "I've got a secret to tell you." He perked right up. I told him that I needed his help. "You're such a big boy now that you can help me out. And I can count on you. So . . ." I explained that his sister was so little that there were many things she couldn't do that he could do. His little chest puffed up with pride. I won his cooperation, as you suggested. Now he even brings me diapers and wipes—his nose pinched dramatically, of course—when his sister has a stinky diaper. He's stopped pinching and biting her.

I got a kick out of him yesterday. I'd put Tricia in her stroller so we could walk to a nearby park when I realized I'd forgotten my house keys. A kid with a dog walked by, and the dog started to stick its nose into Tricia's stroller.

"Hey!" Kent yelled and whipped the stroller behind him. "That's my sister. And nobody touches my sister."

He was so loud, I'm sure the whole neighborhood heard it. But to me, it was one of those pivotal moments in parenting you talk about. We'd gotten over a major hump. Your advice made all the difference.

Michelle, California

Power Points

- All behavior has a purpose.
- Ninety-nine percent of misbehaving kids fall into the attention and power stages.
- Your child's life mantra influences everything she does.
- Kids only misbehave when they have a reason—and their behavior works.

10

The Attention-Getting Kid

What you can do differently to ratchet down your (and their) stress.

Nobody knows attention-seeking kids better than me, because I was one. When I was younger, I had a partial plate in my mouth and could drop three teeth. So I'd drop my teeth and do a family commercial for my brother-in-law, a dentist whose last name was Chall.

"Yup, I went to Dr. Chall," I'd lisp, "and he fixed me right up." I'd have my entire family flat on their backsides, laughing.

When I was a fourth grader, I got sent home from school for sticking my finger down my pants and wiggling it out my fly at some girls. (Wouldn't you have liked to be the mama who had to be in the principal office because of that one? Yes, my mom was a saint.)

When I was a sophomore in high school, I really hated history. So in my world history class, I slid out of my chair, slithered to the back door, opened the door, and crawled right out. I had the whole class laughing hysterically, and poor Mr. Giffen hadn't a clue what was happening.

As I look back at my life, I see threads of attention-seeking running all through it. I'm still prone to attention-getting. I'm a natural entertainer.

When I was on *The View*, I got a standing ovation from both the crowd and the folks in the greenroom as I walked off. Comedian Jon Stewart, who was also in the greenroom and set to go on next, eyed me and said, "Thanks a lot." I took that as the highest form of encouragement.

As a young kid, I was that little attention-getter to the nth degree. To this day, I'm known as the guy who always wears wild socks and a Hawaiian shirt. I've never heard anyone say, "Oh, he's the serious guy with the sport coat and tie," because it wouldn't be true. I go out of my way to be noticed.

I can get any crowd's attention—whether on TV, at a ball game, or in a seminar. As a child and a young man, though, I used that attention-seeking goal to get negative attention. It took encouragement and redirection from key people in my life to turn that attention-seeking into a positive purpose. I became a platform speaker who is able to entertain, inform, encourage, and inspire thousands of people.

Acting Out a Life Theme

We're all actors on the stage of life. We act out our life theme—our perception of ourselves.

All kids are attention-getters—some in a positive way and some in a negative way. How do you know, though, if your child has gone beyond the usual attention-getting of any child to making it his goal to become an attention-getter? Easy. As I've said earlier, check your own emotional response to that child. If you feel provoked and annoyed by him, and you're saying, "You can't do that" to him so much that it's becoming part of your vocabulary, then he's seeking your attention.

For example, let's say Johnny is sitting in class, tapping a pencil or constantly flipping a penny. If the teacher says, "Johnny, that's

All kids are attention-getters.

enough," he'll usually stop. If he doesn't—if he starts tapping that pencil or flipping that penny again—you've got a kid who has a need for attention.

In other words, his life mantra is, *I only count when I have other people's attention*. And he'll act out that life theme by doing goofy things—like making wild birdcalls in class—or getting in other people's faces to provoke action of some kind.

Kids learn patterns early, and the earlier you catch those patterns, the better. As we get older, we are more resistant to change. That's why it's important to catch your child at the earliest goal of misbehavior—attention-getting—before he goes on to the power-driven stage. If a child starts off as an attention-getter and doesn't get the desired results, he will move on to the power-driven stage. Not only is he going to get your attention, he's going to *make you* pay attention to him.

Back to purposive behavior again: all behavior serves a purpose. The 4-year-old who knocks over his 18-month-old baby brother on purpose or breaks your favorite vase is exhibiting purposive behavior. He feels insecure because of this new little special present in your lives, and he's acting out of fear that you're not going to have enough love or attention for him because the baby seems to be getting more attention. After all, both of his grandparents held the baby for 45 minutes each. Your kid knows that because you've taught him how to tell time. *And they hardly paid any attention to me. Well, I'll show them*, he thinks.

So he acts out all his frustration against that sibling anytime your head is turned. You do the traditional thing most parents do. "What is wrong with you?" you say, voice raised. "Leave your brother alone. He's only a baby, and he didn't do anything to you."

All behavior serves a purpose.

But your older child's actions provoked a response and garnered him attention, didn't they? Your kid will only ramp up his behavior if it works. And if he continues on the attention-getting track, he'll eventually move to the power-driven goal. By the time he's 14, he'll be running your house and you'll be pulling your hair out.

What if, instead, you nip that attention-seeking behavior in the bud by engaging your son in conversation and involving him with that baby in a positive way? Giving him privileges and special responsibilities because he's older, and looping him in to care for the baby?

Pull that big brother aside. "I've got to talk to you about your brother. He's such a little kid. He has to take a lot of naps—at least two times a day. You don't take naps anymore, do you? In fact, you're in preschool. And you know something? Your little brother doesn't even know his colors. But you do. What color is this, that? Maybe someday you could teach your brother his colors."

By now your son is feeling special. You're paying attention to him, but it's because of a positive conversation. His little brother isn't looking so bad after all, and his position as firstborn is now secure.

You continue. "I love it when you help Mommy. I always feel so special when you do something kind. Would you run in the bedroom and get your brother a Pampers? Oh, and get the powder too. I'm going to have you put the powder on him this time."

You've effectively taken your son's atten-tion-getting behavior and flipped it toward

Your kid will only ramp up his behavior if it works.

the good, showing him that since he's older, he can actively help with his brother. You've handled his insecurity too—that his sover-eignty as firstborn might be usurped by the invading sibling. You've nipped in the bud his attention-getting behavior before it becomes power-driven behavior. There's no threat anymore, so your child won't ramp up his behavior.

But what most parents do is up the ante. They tell a child not to do something and he does it anyway. So the parent responds, "You've just earned no TV for two days."

The kid says something smart-alecky.

The parent says, "All right, smart guy, make it three days."

Again, all that parent is doing is upping the ante. You might as well throw gas on a fire. Emotions start running high on both sides of the fence. And when they do, your child takes the next step—to becoming power-driven. When a child becomes powerful, his life theme becomes, *Nobody can make me do anything. Nobody is the boss of me. I'm going to live life the way I want to. I'm not going to be stopped by your rules.*

And the war is on, with only respites here and there between the daily skirmishes.

That's why it all comes down to your relationship with your child. As I've heard Josh McDowell say, "Rules without relation-ship lead to rebellion."

They Don't Care What You Know . . .
Until They Know That You Care

When Sande and I were first married, we lived in a dorm, and I was head dorm rat. My mom and dad would come by every once in a while, visit us, and bring us care packages. They were simple things, like a quart of OJ or a box of Saltines. They knew we were living on nothing; we didn't have two nickels to rub together. Why did they bring those packages when they didn't have much themselves? Because they cared.

I know a crusty old University of Arizona football coach, Bill Kirelawich, who barks out orders to his players like a staff sergeant in the Marine Corps. To put it bluntly, he's a great coach and quite a character. He can use some words that you might hear at sea as a conjunction, adverb, adjective, and any other part of speech—all in one afternoon.

I gave him my book *The Way of the Shepherd* because I thought he might enjoy it, since he's a voracious reader and a manager of people. The other day I ran into him again. With a stubby cigar hanging out of his mouth, he said, "Hey, I read your book. I really liked the statement, 'They don't care what you know . . . until they know that you care.'"

I was impressed he could quote it word for word. I walked out of the practice, went home, took the book out, and found the statement. It wasn't one of my main points, yet it had hit home with that coach.

Coach Kirelawich has sent many ballplayers to the NFL. He's very good and as old-school as they come. This guy made all his ballplayers toe the line. The other day he told them, "No matter what it takes, I'm going to make each of you into a football player." And he ran his players hard.

But after practice, I enjoyed watching Coach Kirelawich and his boss, Rich Rodriguez, set up—believe it or not—a water balloon toss. Imagine it—big college football players, 250 to 340 pounds apiece, throwing water balloons at 5 yards, 10 yards, and having to catch the balloon without breaking. After another practice, they did a tug-of-war contest. Another time they did a drill where two or three athletes would pick up another athlete and race to the 50-yard line.

The University of Arizona coaches did those things because they know how important it is to establish a relationship with those players and to have fun. They truly live out the mantra, "They don't care what you know . . . until they know that you care."

Do your kids know that you care? Do they see it in everything you say and do—even when you sometimes have to say and do the hard things?

Caring doesn't mean you bend over and let your kids run over you or that you do things for them that they should do for themselves. Good parenting is like riding the middle of a teeter-totter. If you have two kids who are fairly even-keeled, that teeter-totter works well and is evenly balanced. But if your kids are running from one side to another, challenging each other, then you're going to wear yourself out trying to be that balance point in the middle.

> **Good parenting is like riding the middle of a teeter-totter.**

What you can do

- Seek out your child's opinion.

Your child needs to know her opinion matters. If you're going to paint the house and you're considering the color of her room, ask her what she thinks. So many parents act like horses' tails, having all the answers to life and everything that goes on in their back pocket. They never take the time or even think of asking a kid, "What do you want to do?" or "What do you think we should do?" But when you do ask, what you're saying is, "I value you. You're important to this family. And what you think matters to me."

For example, my son, Kevin, loved to draw. He'd draw on anything—whether it was something he was supposed to draw on or not. So my brilliant wife got an idea. When we were repainting the house, she told Kevin that his room was his to decorate however he liked. He had a blast painting and drawing all over the walls. It became his signature art spot, and we no longer caught him drawing in inappropriate places.

Contrast that with Mandy, another born artist. When her parents were repainting her room, she begged her dad to be able to paint her room herself and got a flat-out no. Her father thought it would look too messy and even called the idea tacky. (Have you figured out that the father was a perfectionistic firstborn?) Imagine his surprise when Mandy and her friends were caught drawing graffiti all over the walls of a local building. While her father went apoplectic at the news, her wise grandpa just said, "Send her over to my place."

When Mandy arrived, her grandpa didn't mention her getting in trouble. He sat in his easy chair and said, "I was thinking about how much your grandmama loved her old cream can from the farm. It would make her smile down from heaven if you'd paint it for me so it could welcome folks who step onto my front porch." That was the best present he could have ever given an artistic girl.

From the cream can, Mandy moved on to turning one of her grandpa's kitchen walls into a restful farm scene, then painted barnlike flourishes around each of his light switches. Sadly, two years later her father still doesn't understand Mandy's talents.

But Mandy and her grandfather have a close relationship, and his house is an artist's dream come true. Once a week, all the older neighbors gather there for a potluck and a look-see at the new artwork, with Mandy as the tour guide. No longer is she seeking attention inappropriately; she's using her skills for the good, to help others. Currently, she's befriending the widowed lady down the street (who just might have her eye on Mandy's grandpa) and painting a flower garden on that woman's kitchen wall.

- Win their cooperation.

When I was a young buck, starting out in the university system as a grad student, my first assignment, as I stated, was to be head resident in a dorm. That particular dorm housed 360 young men. My associate dean of students, Bill Foster, with whom I became close friends as we grew older, gave me a great piece of advice. I've never forgotten it.

"Kevin," he said, "just remember one thing. There's 360 of them and one of you. Learn to win their cooperation."

I followed his advice and was successful.

The next year, the university moved me to a football dorm that housed all football players. The year before, when I was getting my feet wet in the other dorm, the football players had nearly torn the place up and had put the head resident in the hospital. Somebody had smashed him in the face and broken his eye socket.

I remember telling the dean, "I'm not going over there."

He said, "Leman, there's one guy who can go into that hall and straighten that place out. It's you."

So I took the challenge. Did I take a billy club and a whistle? No, I met those kids at the curb, welcomed them to the dorm, and carried their luggage up to their rooms. My staff and I serviced the heck out of those guys. That entire year, there was no damage to the building and practically no fire alarms, which had tortured all the residents the previous years.

Sometimes huffing and puffing and trying to blow the door down like the big bad wolf is the wrong way to go. After all, it didn't work out so well for the wolf, did it?

But you're smarter than that. Service your kids and win their cooperation, and you'll be amazed at how many fewer negative antics you'll see. And your house will be a lot quieter too.

> **Sometimes huffing and puffing and trying to blow the door down like the big bad wolf is the wrong way to go. After all, it didn't work out so well for the wolf, did it?**

So how do you win their cooperation?

For instance, if you have a problem and they might be able to help, run that problem by them. Let's say you realize you need to have your two younger kids in two places at once. Your older daughter has her license and has shown herself to be responsible, even if she does have a sassy attitude. You approach her and say, "I'm wondering if you can help me with something. Your brothers have to be in two places at the same time. Would you be willing to drive one of them for me? If so, I'd really appreciate it."

Your attention-seeking daughter is thinking, *Wow. Mom really trusts me. That feels good.* "Sure," she says.

"Great! That would help a lot. Mark has to go to T-ball and Terry to soccer practice. Which one would you rather take?" you ask.

Now your daughter is thinking, *And she's giving me a choice. Now that's really cool!*

See how it works?

• Allow your child to contribute to the family.

Every child has natural talents and abilities and can contribute. If your 12-year-old son knows more about computers than you do, ask for his help in setting up your bill payments online. Better yet, see if he'd be willing to pay those bills for you once a month. Most 12-year-olds would think it's pretty awesome to be trusted like that. And if he's getting attention and being encouraged because he's contributing to the family, he won't be seeking attention negatively by pestering his younger sister until she cries.

Even your 3-year-old can unload your groceries and stack cans in your pantry. He may do it a lot more slowly than you would, but he'll contribute and have fun doing it.

An 8-year-old can make spaghetti for dinner, thanks to Ragu. It may not be a balanced meal complete with salad and bread, but it'll feed the masses.

Every time your children help and you reward their efforts with a thanks and a smile, you are giving them the attention they crave—in a positive way.

> **Every time your children help and you reward their efforts with a thanks and a smile, you are giving them the attention they crave—in a positive way.**

When you care about someone, you seek out their opinion, you win their cooperation, and you allow them to contribute to your family—before they have to do something to get your attention.

If you focus on those three things, your attention-seeking or powerful children won't be digging their heels in against you. They'll be walking and working alongside you.

Everybody Needs Attention

All of us need to be noticed, and most of us thrive on getting noticed in a positive way.

"Congrats on your promotion," you hear, and you beam.

"That was a special award," someone tells you, and you smile.

Your child needs the same thing. But he needs your encouragement, not your praise.

When your son achieves the Eagle Scout rank, that's a big thing. But your statement shouldn't be, "I'm so proud of you. Look at what you did, Harold. You will be the best Eagle Scout of all. You're going to be a blessing to everybody; yes, you are. I can't wait to call your grandma and tell her the big news!" Such praise is overdone, focused on the child, and heaped on without much thought. It actually does the opposite of what the parent is trying to accomplish. Your smart Eagle Scout knows you're just blathering and that half of what you say is a lie. He knows he isn't going to be the best Eagle Scout. There are a lot of better kids in the running.

What should you say instead? "That has to feel good inside. You worked so hard to accomplish that." Such a statement focuses on the work your young man has done to attain his goal. And it's also more apt to keep your child self-motivated to be an achiever, because it grows his self-worth and informs his life theme. He begins to think, *I can accomplish big things when I work hard*. Kids with life themes like that will take off and fly.

Powerful Ideas That Work

My middle son, Joshua—my sweet, thoughtful child—changed when he started junior high and fell into a group of kids who weren't good for him. Teachers complained about him getting bathroom passes just to get out of class so he could wander down the hallway. He pretended to fall in the hallway, then took a picture on his cell phone from under a girl's skirt and passed it around his group. I found out later it was a dare, but I still couldn't believe he'd done that. That was only the start of things he did to gain the wrong kind of attention at school.

By his second year of junior high, his behavior was driving me crazy. Okay, I admit, it was embarrassing too. Your *Birth Order Book* was the first book I found that was helpful. I met Josh after school one day while his older and younger brothers went home on the bus. We drove to a park where none of his friends would be caught dead (it was a kiddie park), so I knew we wouldn't be interrupted. I asked him if he felt ignored at home, squashed between his little brother, who was always getting attention, and his older brother, Mr. Big-Time Athlete. He hesitated, then admitted yes. That was a long, hard conversation, but we began to realize that the reason he was trying to get attention at school was because he felt left in the dust—like he didn't matter—at home.

Nothing is instant, but things changed that day. My brother took Josh away on a fishing weekend, just the two of them. I picked him up regularly one day a week after school. I was amazed at the difference it made, and Josh seemed happier. The principal's phone calls became fewer and fewer. In fact, I haven't received one for three months now (that's a record in our home with three lively boys). I'm so glad I read your book and found out what my middleborn really needed—to be loved, noticed, and included.

Latricia, New Jersey

──────────── **Power Points** ────────────

- All children seek attention—positively or negatively.

- All behavior serves a purpose. It only continues if it works.
- Seek your kids' opinions, win their cooperation, and allow them to contribute.
- They don't care what you know . . . until they know that you care.

11

Power-Driven or Determined?

*How to know the difference and what
you can do to successfully maneuver
the power surges in your home.*

My granddaughter, Adeline, is a determined kid. When she was 6 years old, her school had a fund-raiser where the children ran laps. All grades competed for first prize, and even though Adeline was only in kindergarten, she won! She ran 17 laps—nearly 30 straight minutes of running. Most kids ran one lap and then decided to walk. Not Adeline. She powered ahead with her best effort.

And that's not the only area in which she shows determination. My wife used to run an antique shop, and she has lots of items from that shop in our garage. When our daughter Krissy was decorating Adeline's bedroom, Krissy and Sande found a perfect chest of drawers for the room. It was antique and lovely.

Krissy took out all the drawers and managed to haul the dresser single-handedly into the room (it was a heavy piece of furniture).

Then she replaced the drawers and filled them up with Adeline's things.

The next day Krissy called me in the late afternoon, frightened. "Dad, I think there are burglars in the house."

"Why do you think that?"

"Because Adeline's dresser is out in the hallway."

Long and short of it, we found out that powerful little Adeline had decided she didn't like the dresser and had pushed it—*by herself*—into the hallway.

Krissy was stunned. "I could hardly push it with the drawers out," she said. So she asked Adeline how she'd gotten the dresser out in the hallway.

Determined little Adeline made a grimace, combined with an "errr," outstretching her arms to show how she pushed it, bit by bit, until the task was done.

Now there's a good example of a kid who's going to become an adult who won't give up until a task is done, no matter how difficult it is. She has already proved it at a young age.

In fact, she's far ahead of her ol' grandpa. I, too, discovered I could do things at a young age. One of the defining moments of my life was when I discovered that I could control classrooms by way of entertainment. I could control people by making other kids laugh. Of course, along the way, I made a lot of teachers very uncomfortable; some even felt threatened and quit after having to teach me. I was a power-driven kid who used humor so others wouldn't mess with me. (It was better than getting decked by a kid who was dared to knock my lights out.)

As a result, everybody liked me. The students, that is. They were rescued from some otherwise dull droning in the classroom when my antics made the class lively. But I never thought of using my attention-getting and power-driven goals for a positive purpose until a spunky teacher pulled me aside in April of my senior year and said, "Did you ever think you could use those skills you have to do something positive in life?"

I thought, *Skills? I've got skills?* It was the first time a teacher had ever told me I had skills.

It was a turning point in my life.

Is It Power—or Determination?

There's a big difference between myself and my granddaughter. Adeline is a determined child—the kind of kid who won't quit until a project is done. She refuses to believe a project can't be done and figures out ways to accomplish it, even if it seems impossible. And the majority of the time, she does accomplish it. I can't wait to see what career track she takes. The power behind her is her levelheaded parents, who have given her the positive attention she needs to develop a balanced but determined attitude.

I, on the other hand, failed at getting attention positively, so I sought it negatively. And when I realized how entertaining my antics were and that they were a good way to get attention, I became powerful. I craved the power and control I received when people laughed, and I became the center of attention. I wanted more and more and more of that attention.

When kids are power-driven, it's like they're thirsty all the time, and not even all the Gatorade in the world will be enough. They see the Big Mac, fries, and Coke meal, and they want not only the whole thing but even the apple pies to go with it!

The other good way to tell if you have a determined kid or a power-driven one is if your child acts differently in one environment than in another. For instance, does your teenager sass you at home but speak kindly to all other figures of authority? Or do your kids behave at Grandma's but morph into holy terrors as soon as they set foot in your living room? There's a big clue right there that something is happening in your relationship.

> **They see the Big Mac, fries, and Coke meal, and they want not only the whole thing but even the apple pies to go with it!**

Hmm, the children are the same. So what is it about your home environment or you as the parental authority that is changing the picture of their behavior? Could it be that two power-driven people in the same household are shorting out the family circuit board?

Taught to Be Powerful

When parents overplay their hand—by overdisciplining a child, by acting out the "I'm your mom/dad. I'm the one in charge here" role—they kick off the goal of power in a child. Whenever there's a powerful kid, there's a powerful parent in the home. And two powerful people in one home will always butt heads.

Think about it for a minute. When was the last time you butted heads with your powerful kid? Would you admit you have a stubborn streak as wide as your son's or daughter's?

It's no wonder that child is considering you with narrowed eyes, waiting to leap like a tiger onto prey. Your relationship has become an exercise in whose will is going to win out. Since powerful people have an agenda to control, that means in any relationship, one person is going to be the controller and the other the controllee. So what happens when both want to be the controller? The wires cross and there are sparks zapping all over that circuit board.

When you come head-to-head with your powerful child, what do you usually say—if not aloud, then in your mind? *You can't say that to me (or do that to me), because I'm the parent here.* But if you truly are in authority, you're going to be smarter than that kid. You're going to choose not to do battle, since fighting would be an act of cooperation to escalate the battle further.

Members of a family innately know each other's soft spots. They're like boxers sparring in a practice ring. If you practice sparring with a partner long enough, you get to know his moves. Professional boxers will change sparring partners for that reason.

It takes a mature parent to admit, *My son who worries me is a lot like me.* But that's also a smart parent.

Keep in mind that we parents tend to project our unfulfilled dreams and wishes on our kids, so if we see our child going a different direction than what we've planned in our heads, it's a double worry: (1) she's not doing what you think she should do, what you know she should do, and what you want her to do; and (2) she'll end up with the same frustrations and war wounds you've had in your life.

> **It takes a mature parent to admit, *My son who worries me is a lot like me.***

I'm going to say something shocking: get good at being a worse parent. Don't try so hard to do so many things for your kids. Don't be the one to solve their problems. It's better to say, "I don't have a clue what the answer to that question is, but google it and let me know what you find." That's much healthier for you and your child than telling him. It keeps the tennis ball of discovery on his side of life's net.

When a powerful person runs into another powerful person, neither likes it. The fur flies, but both take a step back out of respect because they realize the other person is not going to be easily fooled, manipulated, or talked into something they don't believe.

If you were taught as a child to be powerful, and you're playing the power game as an adult in your home, it's time to reflect on your background—what made you progress from attention-seeking to power-driven. Until you help yourself, you can't help your child.

Two powerful people will never be able to coexist peacefully.

Discipline or Punishment?

Good discipline strives to teach a valuable lesson. Punishment says, "I'm going to make you feel really bad for what you did. So take this . . ."

Discipline is a gentle but firm way of setting your kid straight on an issue. Believe it or not, every time you do that in a calm, reasoned manner, your stock goes up in your kid's eyes. To use your kid's terminology, "Hey, you don't mess with my mom and dad. They're not fools. You can't just tell them anything. They won't fall for it."

Are you a parent who commands—note I didn't say *demands*—respect?

> **Discipline is a gentle but firm way of setting your kid straight on an issue.**

Most people say that if you discipline a child, it needs to be done as close to the infraction as possible, timewise. But that isn't always true, especially with older children. Sometimes, parent, you have to wait. If the kid smart-mouths you in the morning, you wait until after school, when he says, "Okay, it's time to go to Sam's house."

Then you pull the rug out from under him. "Honey, I'm sorry, but you aren't going anywhere tonight."

I can guarantee you'll get a dropped jaw, some exclamations flying, and/or a major blowout. That child will be angry.

"But Mom, we have to pick him up to go to Little League with us!"

So you explain that you're not going to Little League and that he's going to have to call Sam to explain why he can't give him a ride.

Or if he's older, he says, "But Mom, I told Todd we'd be at the movie theater at 7:00, and the girls we've been trying to get to go out with us will be there too."

Don't fall for the boo-hoo lines. Your son won't be a happy camper, but neither are you, because of how he dissed you in the morning. Don't back down, or you'll lose all the ground you gained.

"I understand you're mad and disappointed," you tell him, "but you can't imagine how disappointed and upset I was this morning when you said to me . . ."

You have to understand that your powerful kid is in a contest of wills with you over who is in authority over whom. Kids who have already moved from attention to power are those who are discouraged—life isn't working out the way they thought it should, so they've ramped up their powerful behavior. Kids at the power-driven level will stay there forever, stirring things up and making chaos out of your home and family life, as long as it pays off for them.

Now that you know that, what will you do in your next power struggle?

If you back down, you reward the behavior. If you stand firm and continue to stand firm, you provide a negative consequence to the powerful behavior.

Give your kid credit for being as smart as he is.

He'll figure things out.

Turning a Powerful Kid Around

A father talked with me, tears streaming down his cheeks, about his concern for his 12-year-old son. He was the class bully and always causing trouble at school and everywhere else he went. He never studied, never completed homework, and argued with his parents and siblings. He was the spark that turned their home into a smoking bomb. The father had tried punishment—taking his Xbox away, grounding him. Nothing worked.

His son shrugged and had the attitude of "Do what you want; it doesn't bother me at all."

That's because a powerful kid won't give you the satisfaction of letting on that anything you do would bother him. He's saying, "I don't care."

So I walked the dad through this conversation, which he ended up having with his son:

"Son, you're in junior high now. I don't know what you plan on doing in life, what kind of car you plan on driving, what section of town you're going to live in, or what kind of job you'll have. Those things will have a lot to do with how you apply yourself at school and work, and how you get along with other people.

"I love you. I'm your dad. I'd take a bullet for you. But as your dad, I'm worried. It seems more important for you to show others that you're right and everybody else is wrong than it is to do what you need to do in order to be successful in life. I'm not so sure you're not going to be one of the guys at the car wash, washing cars the rest of your life. Maybe you think that would be cool. What you aspire to be. And you'd make enough money to buy a pack of cigarettes.

"I want you to take a look around this house. It didn't come without hard work from your mom and me. You're only 12. You've only got six more years to serve in this jail that you find so unfair to you. You can serve the rest of your time with a smile, and we'll smile back. Or you can make things rough on yourself and everybody in this home.

"For whatever reason, you're getting your jollies out of trying to control the entire family, and you live to antagonize your sister. But it came to me the other day that, most likely, you and your sister will be in each other's weddings someday."

Kid: "Yeah, she is my sister."

"I was thinking, too, about how you treat your little brother. I know he can be a real pest sometimes, but I think I just put two and two together. I could be wrong on this, and I'd love to hear what you think. I figure you put your brother down all the time to make yourself feel better because you see him as a threat. But let me ask you. What kind of grades do you get in math? And what does your brother struggle with in school more than any other subject?"

Kid: "Math. He's stupid."

"I thought we were making progress, and here you say he's stupid. You could have stopped at 'math.' You didn't have to add that he's stupid. But there's something in you that makes you automatically put your brother down. I'm only the dad here, but if I told you the number of times your brother has come to me, crying his eyes out because he doesn't feel like you love him, you might be surprised. Do you remember in fifth grade when you got in so much trouble with your mother because you beat the tar out of a kid who called your brother names?"

Kid: "Yeah." A little smirk appears.

"Then tell me the truth right now, and look me in the eyes. Do you love your brother?"

Kid: "Yeah." He ducks his head a little.

"Then do you really have to put him down to make yourself feel better?"

Kid: "I guess not."

"I know I can't make you into something you're not. But I believe in my heart that you know the right thing to do. Tomorrow we're going to start over again with a clean slate. I hope and pray for your sake that it goes better than today. I hope you're willing to give it a try."

Then I told that dad to hug his kid and tell him again that he loved him.

What did I walk that father through? How to tell his kid in plain, simple terms about the realities of life without setting off his defenses. Remember that this dad was talking to a member of the hormone group. Adolescents are weird by nature, and everything is exaggerated at this stage in life. They talk in "always" and "never": "You always do this." "You never let me do that." They speak in black-and-white and absolutes.

Also, the dad was throwing his son a bone to think about: "Most likely, you and your sister will be in each other's weddings someday."

The entire focus of the conversation was moving from the negative side of the attention-getting, power-driven goals to the positive side.

Look for positive behavior.

I also told the dad to look for positive behavior. The very next day, that kid could have said something snotty to his brother, but he said something nice instead. The father pulled the older brother aside later and said, "I was really pleased to watch what you did today. I could almost feel you were going to give your brother a cheap shot. I'm glad you didn't and that you're learning it's a choice. Son, you made the right choice. Made me feel so good as a dad that you're maturing and making the right decisions."

The father rewarded his son with positive attention to curb his attention-seeking, and also began the journey of helping his son learn how to turn his power-driven behavior into something positive.

What you can do

• Don't set up your child.

Here's what I mean. A well-meaning parent takes his 5-year-old kid to Walmart to look at toys a couple of days before Thanksgiving. The father is thinking, *What a smart parent I am. This way I can find out what kind of toys my kid likes so I can shop the sales for Christmas.* He's patting himself on the back.

What does the 5-year-old want? Everything.

Why? Because he's 5 years old, and that means he will naturally have a short attention span and poor impulse control. Even more, delay-of-gratification skills are null and void at age 5. Those things will hopefully be fine-tuned as he matures.

So that father unwittingly walks himself and his son right into a power struggle. Too bad there isn't a sign at Walmart in the toy section: "Attention: You're About to Enter a Danger Zone."

The kid doesn't fall for the dad's line, "We're just seeing what toys you like so we can tell Aunt Anita what you'd like for Christmas." To him, Christmas is abstract, and those weeks away might as well be a millennium and a star system away.

And how will he respond if he's a powerful kid? He's about to let the whole store know exactly what he thinks about walking out without a boatload of those toys.

Parents need to think before they speak and act (as hard as that is to do sometimes). Otherwise they set up situations that allow their kid's power to flourish even more.

- Anticipate the start of the battle.

The best predictor of future behavior is what's happened before. That means we need to be aware of those checkered flags in life that will start the kid's power racing and know not even to get close. We need to anticipate what will happen, especially if it's a regular power struggle that happens often.

Parents need to think before they speak and act.

For example, if it sparks a battle to tell your 10-year-old he has to eat his oatmeal because it's good for him, why go there? There are more things in the world to eat for breakfast than oatmeal, aren't there? I know one child who only eats dinner foods for breakfast. She hates breakfast foods, and she's lactose-intolerant, which cuts out a lot of them anyway.

So who made you the authority on what a kid has to eat for breakfast, as long as what he eats gives him good fuel for his brain and body?

Instead, casually say to your child as he's chowing down on an after-school snack, "I need to go to the grocery store in the next day or two. What kind of things would you like me to get that you might like to eat for breakfast?" Then, smart parent that you are, you purchase the healthy items on your kid's list. That way he gets what he wants to eat, and you know he's eating healthy, which makes you smile. You've also halted the power struggle by anticipating the battle and coming up with Plan B.

The best predictor of future behavior is what's happened before.

Why not avoid those areas in which you've had trouble in the past?

Avoiding is different than placating. When you placate, you give in so the kid will shut up. That only tells him he's on the right path for getting what he wants.

But you can gently take your powerful buzzard by the beak in a calm, controlled, pre-thought-out manner that will leave your child scratching his head, wondering what's up with Mom or Dad.

Then you've got 'em right where you want 'em.

• Respond rather than react.

Disarming your power-driven child will only happen if you change your thinking, your approach, and the words you choose to say, and you respond rather than react.

For those of you who are married, it's very important that you and your spouse get on the same page and stay on the same page. If only one of you is consistent and the other is all over the map, your power-driven child will ramp up her power, and she'll use it to divide you. Both of you have to stick to your guns in a united effort.

> **Disarming your power-driven child will only happen if you change your thinking, your approach, and the words you choose to say, and you respond rather than react.**

Instead of reacting in emotion, saying, "Why on earth would you do something like that?" try this instead: "You must really have been frustrated or angry to do that. Do you want to talk about it?"

Such an approach doesn't diss the kid, but it does put that ball of responsibility directly in her court, not yours.

If you get the brick-wall response—in other words, you might as well be talking to one—let it go for now. That kid may be absolutely silent but is saying loudly, "I don't give a rip what you think or say." So, parent, back off. When you aren't pushing her direction, she'll come yours. It's an amazing relational phenomenon.

Responding rather than reacting also means you don't take any cheap shots. You don't make the kid wallow in his attitude or mistake. Like the dad in this chapter who shot straight with his son, you allow the child to start fresh the next day.

You know your child's trigger points, just as he knows yours. Certain body language and expressions will set him off. Keep in mind that you're the power source. So in order to power him down, you need to power yourself down.

Take these responses out of your vocabulary:

- "What is wrong with you?"
- "We never had this problem with your brother."
- "Really. You're acting like a 3-year-old."

If you keep yourself out of your child's grasp by not allowing yourself to react emotionally, there's a lesser chance you're going to be tricked or coerced into saying or doing anything that sparks the whole situation all over again.

Your kid will power up if you power up.

Your kid will power down if you power down.

I guarantee it.

Powerful Ideas That Work

My husband and I both changed jobs in the same year. I could no longer pick Becky up from her grade school, and Andi, her little sister, had to go to preschool rather than staying home with me since I no longer worked from home.

Becky was a great student, but her grades started slipping. I got notes that she was being disruptive in class. One day she set a fire in her homeroom teacher's garbage can. When I asked her why she did it, she said, "To get a laugh." I remembered what you'd said in a parenting seminar about kids who sought attention—that if they didn't get it, they moved on to make you pay attention. Wow. That was us.

My husband and I decided to juggle work schedules so one of us could drop off the girls in the morning and the other one could pick them up. I'm hoping my boss will soon approve my request to work a day from home. It's not a perfect setup—neither is life!—but we're working on it.

Tammy, New Hampshire

Power Points

- There's a difference between *determined* and *power-driven*.
- Power begets power.
- Identify the trigger points, and don't set up the battle.
- Respond rather than react.

12

You're the Adult, They're the Children

That powerful child has everything to do with you, your background, and your views of parenting.

Having kids is a little like having a puppy. There, I said it. In previous books I've tried not to say it, but the older I get, the more I see the similarities.

With puppies, you have to take time for training; otherwise, they'll pee on your Berber carpet.

But in order to train them, you have to pay attention to what they're doing. When Fido starts to get in that position on the floor where you know he's going to go potty, you pick him up as quickly as you can, take him outside, and plop him in a grassy area.

He gets the idea and goes potty.

You pat his head, then give him a treat.

Pretty soon the dog understands that, as convenient as it is to go potty on the Berber carpet, the carpet doesn't really have good smells. But outside, on the grass, there are all kinds of wonderful smells. Even better, when he goes potty on the grass, he gets a treat afterward.

Soon the process becomes a learned habit. Our dog, Rosie, is 9 years old, but she still gets a treat when she goes outside to do her business. Lately, just to show what a smart dog she is, she's been waking me up at 1:30 a.m. and then again at 4:40 a.m., wanting to go outside. I take her outside and give her a treat.

My wife, who thinks she's a better psychologist than I am, says, "Leemie, she's workin' ya."

Funny how Rosie goes to my side of the bed, because she knows that I'll get up and Sande won't.

She probably is working me. Rosie looks around and decides, *Hey, I want a treat. If I wake up that fat guy, he'll open the door, and I'll go out, pretend to do my business, and get a treat when I come back in.*

Only I'm not quite that dumb. When she stands at the door and looks at me, then won't go out the door, I've got her number. She really doesn't have to go; she *is* just working me.

So I don't give her a treat, and I go back to bed.

Ain't Got No Respect

Have you ever been around an unruly dog, one that jumps up on you, climbs all over you, and scratches you? It's not a fun experience. Kids who aren't brought up to be respectful, don't have respect for others' property, and have a mouth on them aren't fun to be around either.

That's why it's important for parents to be parents and to take time for training their children. Mutual respect should be enforced at all times. Powerful children are not allowed to order their mother, father, sister, or brother around. People should follow the Golden Rule at all times—treat others the way you'd want to be treated.

I love watching my grandchildren, Conner and Adeline, when they meet people. They're very polite, saying, "Thank you" and "Nice to meet you." They're kind, considerate, and fun to be around.

That's because our daughter Krissy and her husband, Dennis, have made it a priority to train their children in the way they should go, and they provide an environment of mutual respect, kindness, and balanced discipline when it is needed.

You see, behavior is learned. You acclimate to whatever environment you're in.

I had a professor friend who could never get up by himself; his wife had to wake him up because he'd sleep through his alarm. Yet when he traveled, he'd take along a little Westclox fold-up alarm clock that clicked before it dinged. Every time, he'd wake up with the soft click.

> **Behavior is learned. You acclimate to whatever environment you're in.**

Your child, too, will acclimate to whatever environment he's in. If he knows that Mom and Dad will bail him out, he'll get himself into a lot of situations and then act helpless. With Mom and Dad running interference, he becomes more and more powerful in his behavior, yet weaker in his personality and less able to deal with life on his own.

If Mom and Dad rigidly control a child's life, not allowing him to even make a mistake, then he will find ways to rebel against that authority, whether quietly or openly.

But why would parents choose either to let their children run all over them or to control their children's lives so rigidly they can barely breathe?

It's so much easier to evaluate other people's kids, isn't it, and to be blinded by your own?

How you parent has everything to do with the way you grew up, and your own screenplay that you developed as a result. Now your kids are taking their emotional notes from you.

When Do You Count?

I have a question for you. If you had to complete the statement, "I only count when . . ." what would you say?

Remember that all of us tend to act out whatever our worldview and our birth order tell us. So many of us believe the lie that we only count when we achieve, or win the prize, or serve others. These opinions were reinforced within the social context of our family as we grew older.

If you're the responsible one in your family, most likely there's a reason for it. You are a firstborn. When your parents wanted something done, they didn't call in Little Missikins. In fact, if you'd asked her to point north, she'd only have a one in four chance of getting it right. But you, with your competitive spirit combined with a tad of perfectionism, stayed up all night studying for a chemistry exam. And that artwork you created for your science project never did measure up to what you thought it should be.

Let's face it: you're good at finding flaws in others, but you're much rougher on yourself. In fact, you distinctly remember confiding to a girlfriend at lunch during your senior year that you felt lucky to have received such a high grade on your English test. You had a hard time accepting that you were such a good student, because a little voice inside you said you could have done better.

"Rest and relaxation" is not your middle name. If you're honest with yourself, *driven* describes you, doesn't it? And no wonder. Your dad was always talking about how proud he was of you. He insisted you apply to the most prestigious university in the United States, even though going there took most of his retirement money. Or perhaps your dad was determined you were going to win the Cy Young Award for the best baseball pitcher.

You heard your parents talking about you, and the ante was upped.

Your Growing-Up Years

Did you grow up in a home where your parents told you exactly what to do and when to do it, and they threatened you with dire consequences if you didn't do what they said? If you grew up with two parents who couldn't even agree if the sky was blue, then you got a devastating double dose of power-mongering.

Or did you grow up in a home where you got away with anything, and there were never any consequences?

What life themes did you form as a result?

I only count when I do what I'm supposed to do—when I make others happy.

I only count when I'm in charge.

The life themes you've developed have everything to do with how you parent your own children.

Does your child only count if they score that basket? If they win a national merit scholarship? If they get into a prestigious school? Or do they count because they are a unique creation of a very creative God and have talents and abilities to offer the world to make it a better place?

What life themes did you form as a result?

If you had a lousy relationship with your mom or dad, guess who will pay for it? Those close to you in your own home now. You'll be on a short fuse, grow angry easily, and be prone to power struggles with the child most like you.

If you were an attention-getting child who moved on to become a power-driven child, you're probably the parent who butts heads the most with your powerful child. Powerful kids don't like other powerful people, but they do respect them.

If you were rigidly controlled by your parents, you'll tend to be more of an authoritarian parent.

If you lived in the anything-goes home, you'll tend to be more of a permissive parent.

We always say we'll never parent like our parents did, yet we make the same mistakes they do—over and over—unless we make an active choice to be and to act different.

The Authoritarian Parent: "Mother/Father Knows Best"

We adults are creatures of habit. We assume that since we are adults, we know more than our children. That makes us superior and them inferior . . . or so the reasoning goes. We know what's best for our kids, so we hold the parental hammer of authority above their heads. It's called the authoritarian view of parenting, and it creates tyrants who strive to put some of the power back in their own court.

Authoritarian parents are as headstrong as their children. They return power for power. The authoritarian stance may work when your kids are young and can be controlled, but watch out when they grow up. They'll rebel in more ways than you can imagine.

Most of child rearing is based on superior/inferior relationships:

- "Eat it. It's good for you."
- "Don't lean back in your chair; you're going to break your neck."
- "Get your shoes on. The bus is coming, and you'll be late."

What is that parent saying? Adults are bigger than and thus better than children. That's the traditional view of parents. For example, in 1960, when Kennedy was president of the United States, men were considered better than women, and women better than children.

That meant it was okay to embarrass the heck out of a kid in order to accomplish your purposes. "Johnny, Mrs. Smith has just given you a great gift, and you should say, 'Thank you.'"

> **Authoritarian parents are as headstrong as their children. They return power for power.**

You are the best teacher of your child. The question is, what exactly are you teaching her? If you're always telling your kid what to do, making decisions for her, hovering over her, that's pretty disrespectful. Your child will see that as a put-down—and rightfully so.

In a democratic society, if you have the right to put me down, what right do I have? To put you down.

No wonder a powerful adult begets a powerful child.

It's true that without you, your child couldn't buy her own underwear. But then again, someday that child may be the one buying you Depends.

The Permissive Parent: "Whatever You Want, Dear"

The permissive method of parenting tends to create one thing—tyrants. If you have a demanding child, it's likely because you (or your spouse, if you're married) are a permissive parent. You do everything within your power to keep your little power-hungry sucker happy. You give her the car keys even though she's had two speeding tickets.

But as I said in my book *Have a New Kid by Friday*, an unhappy child is a healthy child. There are times your powerful child should be unhappy, because he acted inappropriately and disrespectfully and you want to curb his powerful nature. If he is to have a chance of living a happy life, he has to figure out he isn't the center of the universe. Life isn't all about him. Other people's ideas and opinions are worthwhile; he can learn from them.

One upset mom told me that her son wasn't liked by his peers. As she explained further, I could see why. The kid sounded like a powerful brat. Honestly, who would want to be friends with a kid like that?

I said, "This sounds like a teachable moment for your son. Someone needs to bring to his attention why other kids don't like him. If he doesn't know, he can't have the opportunity to make a change."

The mom was incensed. "How dare you! My son is just fine. It's all the other kids who have a problem."

No, lady, I thought. *You are your son's problem.*

Mama Bear needed to stop protecting Baby Bear's tail and making excuses for him. Until then, no progress could ever be made.

In my experience, many enabling moms who are ultraprotec-
tive and allow themselves to be controlled and manipulated by
their powerful children have been hurt by life themselves. They
are wounded doves and have often experienced abuse—in their
growing-up years or perhaps in a current or previous marriage.

Permissive parents are the ones who wring their hands and
drag their rebellious child to a shrink at $225 an hour so he can
be labeled with "oppositional defiant disorder" to excuse his behavior. Whereas what they really need to do is to take the bull by
the horns and talk to the kid themselves.
"Son, there is some common ground that
we must all walk on in this family. We
must be respectful and civil to each other.
The reality is, you're 18 years old. You
can find yourself an apartment and do
whatever you want to do. But as long

> **Mama Bear needed to stop protecting Baby Bear's tail and making excuses for him.**

as you're living under this roof, you are not going to talk disrespectfully to anyone in this house, and you will live under our
guidelines."

Parents today seem to have a high need to be liked by their
children. Others go out of their way to make themselves "cool"
in hopes that their kid will like them. But think for a minute how
stupid that is. Your child can and will have many friends in his
lifetime. But he will only have one or two parents.

You, parent, are the key to your child's success. If you allow your
child to unleash his power, he'll be like a great white shark devouring his prey. You won't be able to feed him enough. Powerful kids
feed off of situations where they are the winner—which means,

of course, that someone else is the loser. This wreaks havoc with the entire family.

The Authoritative Parent: The Balanced View

Children may not always like their parents, but they long for someone who will draw the guidelines, since guidelines mean safety. Without guidelines and boundaries, the child feels insecure. As adults, we've lived longer and have experienced more than our kids. It doesn't mean our kids are less worthy, but they haven't experienced as many consequences for their actions as we have.

One person isn't better than another, but as a parent, you agree that you are charged with a whole different set of responsibilities. If you don't think that's true, take a look at the difference between the way that minors and adults who commit the same crime are treated.

So you're the adult here; act like one. Be the parent you need to be. If you don't understand that basic principle, then life will not go well for you as a parent or for your child, either now or in the future.

When you're an authoritative parent, you realize your role is to be in proper authority over your children. Because you love them, you provide them with a home, food, security, education, and some of the amenities of life. You stay up with them at night when they're sick, you clean up their doo-doo, and you pick them up when they call you from places where they don't want to be . . . but somehow ended up there.

> **Your role is to be in proper authority over your children.**

First John 5:19 says we're children of God. And though God is the supreme authority, he's not an authoritarian who gives out edicts and tells us what we have to do. He gives free choice (which gets us in trouble sometimes). But God also isn't a permissive parent who says, "Oh, that's okay. Anything goes."

As parents, instead of uttering almighty edicts from above, we have to give our children age-appropriate choices. Sometimes they may choose wisely, other times not wisely. And with those choices come consequences—for good or for ill.

If your child's behavior works, he'll keep doing it . . . until it no longer reaps rewards.

A Solid Foundation

My lovely wife, Mrs. Uppington, would tell you I'm not very handy around the house. In fact, I'm still trying to memorize the names of the tools so when she tells me what she needs, I can bring her the right one. Yet, since I've walked the earth for six decades, even I know that a building needs a solid foundation. If the foundation isn't right, the whole building is off.

Years ago, as a child, I learned a song with the words, "The wise man built his house upon the rock . . . and the foolish man built his house upon the sand." And we all know the story of the three little pigs. Only one of those piggies was smart enough to build his house out of bricks. It took him longer, but it was well worth it.

The society we live in today is a dangerous one. There are plenty of big bad wolves out there that will devour your child without batting an eye.

What kind of foundation are you giving your kids? Sand? Straw? Twigs? Or cement blocks? If you use anything other than cement, it's not a good idea. I know that because Mrs. Uppington, the mechanic, told me. She even proved it to me while she was laying brick around the house. I saw it with my own two eyes as I sipped a can of Pepsi.

So what does your child want the most?

- To feel valued.
- To be loved unconditionally.
- To be taken seriously.
- To contribute to your family.

Those are the foundations that are like cement blocks: firm and there to stay for a lifetime.

What kind of parent do you tend to be now? Authoritarian? Permissive? How might you change to be that balanced, authoritative parent you need to be—for your own welfare and for your child's?

Powerful Ideas That Work

I had no idea how much my experience with my abusive father has impacted my relationship with my son until last year. Hal had always been a tough kid to control, and it didn't help when my husband and I divorced. Then Hal hardly ever saw his father. He got more and more disrespectful toward me and called me names. I took it, and he dished out more.

Then I heard you talk about how women who were abused when they were growing up often own up to responsibility that isn't theirs, and that I wasn't put on this earth to be somebody's doormat. I took a stand and told my son that as long as he lived in my home, he would act respectfully toward me. He looked at me, shocked, and called me a name I won't repeat. I told him to leave. After he'd slept a couple nights at a friend's house, he showed up back at home and apologized.

It's been three months since he moved back in. He no longer blames me for his father leaving, and I don't see him as a reflection of his father. For both of us, that's a good start.

Marilee, Wyoming

──────────── **Power Points** ────────────

• Behavior is learned.

• You tend to say and do the same things as good ol' Mom and Dad did to you (even though you told yourself you'd never say or do those things to your kids).

• Be the authoritative parent you need to be.

13

What Kind of Kid Do You Want?

*Win-win suggestions to get you from
where you are to where you want to be.*

While driving down my street in Arizona one day, I spotted something that resembled a small rock . . . but it was moving. Getting out of the car, I moved closer and realized it was a good-sized desert tortoise. So I did the only thing that a grandpa could do, and with great joy: I took him to Conner, my grandson, who loves desert tortoises.

Conner was ecstatic. Within seconds he was out in the backyard, building a place for the critter and playing with him. Conner named him George and cared for him as if he were a king. The next two days were blissful.

Then I got a call from Krissy. "Uh, Dad, did you see the sign in our neighborhood? It says 'Lost Tortoise.'"

I was thinking, *Oh no. Betcha anything the tortoise I found is this person's.* "Oh, honey," I said to Krissy, "Conner will be heartbroken. But you have to do the right thing."

Poor Conner. He was 6 years old at the time.

Krissy—being the balanced, mature mom that she is, thoroughly schooled in the Leman technique of being an authoritative parent instead of an authoritarian or permissive parent—thought through how to present the concept to Conner.

She told him, "Conner, there's something I want to tell you. I want you to take a ride with me in the car." And she drove him right past that "Lost Tortoise" sign.

Conner's face said it all: "Uh-oh" and "Nuh-uh." He knew it had to do with his tortoise, and he didn't want any part of giving George to anybody for any reason.

So Krissy said gently, "You know, Conner, it's probably that person's tortoise that Grandpa found."

Conner was grief-stricken.

If Krissy had pulled the authoritarian parent stance, she'd have said, "Conner, that's not your tortoise. It belongs to another guy. We need to call that number and give the guy his turtle."

That's like grabbing a kid by the scruff of the neck and making his decision for him, without giving him any say. Just announcing the almighty-from-above parental dictate.

If she had pulled the permissive parent stance, she'd have said, "Oh, honey, I'm sure that can't be the same tortoise. Even if he is, he's your tortoise now."

That would be like pushing all the dirt in your house under the rug and pretending it's not there—until the seeds from your bird food sprout into plants through the rug.

No, instead, Krissy was an authoritative parent. She was the parental figure, but she put the responsibility in Conner's court. She told him what the facts were—about how and where I found the tortoise, that they'd only had it for a few days, and that there was a guy in the neighborhood who'd had a tortoise for many years. Then she left it up to him to decide what to do. All she said was, "Conner, you gotta do the right thing."

Conner took a day to think it over. He could have done whatever he wanted to do, but he chose to do the right thing.

The guy lived two streets away. He was ecstatic when he got the phone call and said, "We'll be right over." It wasn't long before two people showed up—a young grandpa and a young man. They were so excited to see their tortoise again . . . only it wasn't their tortoise. George was bigger.

Everyone had assumed it would be the guy's tortoise. In fact, the other guy was so sure that, because he knew he'd be coming to a little kid's house, he'd brought a little box turtle for Conner, and also one for his sister, Adeline.

So Conner not only did the right thing but got to keep George.

Have you ever seen a kid who has demolished a peanut butter and jelly sandwich but is still sporting the remainders of that lunch all over his face? Or a kid who's just had a fudge sundae? Then you know what George looks like when he eats his favorite lunch. Once a year our very ugly cactus bears the most gorgeous red fruit, and tortoises love to eat it. It's a hilarious thing to watch. I don't know who's smiling more in the photo I have: George with the red dripping off his face, or Conner holding him.

Conner took a day to think it over.

Every time I see Conner with that tortoise, I smile for three reasons: for the fun Conner is having; for his mom, who offered a teachable moment; and for Conner, because he chose to do the right thing.

Peek Down Your Child's Road . . .

Ask yourself this question: "Where in life would I like my child to be X number of years from now as he leaves my nest, in regard to his work ethic, attitude, integrity, moral character, and behavior?"

If you could choose five character traits or adjectives for your child to have, what would they be? Take a few minutes to list them.

- _____
- _____
- _____
- _____
- _____

If that's the kind of child you want, how are you going to get from here to there? From your 18-month-old or toddler or 5-year-old to an 18-year-old who is out of your feathered nest?

If you want an honest child, how will you work on that attribute?

If you want your child to be kind and thoughtful of others, how will you teach him that?

If you want a hardworking, diligent, finish-what-she-started kid, how will you get there?

If you want a responsible child who becomes a contributing member to society, how will you accomplish that?

Respected leader Stephen Covey always said, "Start with the end in mind."

That means if you want an honest child, you first make sure you are honest, and your child sees you being honest in both little and big things. You return extra change that a checker mistakenly gives you. You tell your boss the truth on the phone about why you're running late to work. After all, you are your child's number one role model, and ears are listening and eyes are watching.

If you want your child to be kind and thoughtful, then you be kind and thoughtful. You go the extra mile for others. You provide opportunities for your child to give to others: "Let's bake some cookies for the neighbors today, shall we? They're having a hard time, and I know it will cheer them all up." You serve on a Saturday morning in a soup kitchen.

If you want your child to be hardworking and finish what she starts, then you work hard. You start projects around the house and finish them—even better, with your child's help. You say, "That A on your science project must feel so awesome. You worked really hard on a tough topic."

If you want a responsible child, then you be responsible. You give him responsibilities, whether it's feeding a goldfish, taking out the trash, or cleaning his room. And you teach him that he won't always like to do the responsibilities, but they need to be done anyway.

An important thing to remember is that every child is unique. That means what worked with child number one won't work with child number two. That's because, as I've said earlier in this book, the secondborn child will take the opposite way of the firstborn since he can't compete on the same level.

Stephen Covey always said, "Start with the end in mind."

Powerful kids will go one of two directions—either they'll become self-centered, hedonistic suckers who will sap the life out of others, taking instead of giving, or they'll become kids with determination and balance who have discovered that they're not the center of the universe.

Kids who are powerful have an insatiable appetite for attention, power, and control. They can become powerful adults who devour everything and everyone in their path. If they see you as weak, they'll run over you.

Or they can become adults on a trajectory to make a difference in the lives of those on this planet. They'll take high school and college in stride because they have a parent or parents behind them who believe in them and act as that circuit breaker on their life experiences. These kids will have a hunger to learn and to excel, and they'll be kind to others, standing up for the downtrodden. They are the kids who can accomplish a great deal in life for the good.

That can be your powerful kid.

The Right Ingredients

I'm not much of a cook, but I do know something from my gourmet wife—if you want a dish to turn out right, you have to put in the right ingredients, or else it won't taste anything like it's supposed to. I can't tell you how many times Sande has sent me to the grocery store with strict instructions, such as, "Get a devil's food cake mix, and it has to be Duncan Hines. No other brand."

Just like a good recipe, there are foundational things—certain basic ingredients—that you have to put into your kid:

- encouragement but not praise
- discipline but not punishment
- guidelines but not editorials or dictates
- grace and not bone-digging (more on that in the next chapter).

Not only do the ingredients have to be in there, they have to be prepared right and baked at the right temperature. Pie doesn't taste very good if the crust doesn't have the right ingredients or it's underbaked, because it's the foundation of the pie.

So let's take a look again at that list you made. For each character trait/adjective, make a separate sheet of paper that looks like this:

Character trait/adjective

What it looks like now in my child:

What I'd like to see in my child:

Ideas for getting from here to there:

Be completely honest. This paper is just for you (and your spouse, if you're married). In the "What it looks like now in my child" section, if your child is really struggling in that area, write down how and why you think he's struggling.

Move on to "What I'd like to see in my child." This is your chance to dream, to imagine your child 5, 10, 15, 20 years down the road with that quality. How would it affect his life?

Under "Ideas for getting from here to there," jot down ways you could help your child develop this quality, starting today. Jot down little things, big things, practical steps, brainstorms.

Let's take the character trait of honesty for an example. Here's what your page might look like:

Honesty

What it looks like now in my child:

- He stole 10 bucks out of his grandpa's wallet last week.

  He wants some money of his own? He's a sneaky, dishonest kid?

- He lied when I asked him if he'd fed the dog.

  He didn't feel like it? He felt bad because he forgot and didn't know how to get out of it?

- He said he wasn't feeling well when I asked him to help me clean the house. Half an hour later, I found him playing video games and eating Cheetos and a Snickers bar.

  He lied? He was lazy? He was downright disobedient? He wanted to be in control of his schedule, and I was harping too much?

- He told a friend that he couldn't play, but he could. He just didn't want to play with that boy.

  Maybe his friends are changing, and he doesn't know how to tell the kid that? Maybe he felt like being lazy? Maybe he was tired and just wanted some time alone?

Focusing in on the possibilities for the child's behavior disengages your emotions (often anger, in the case of a powerful child's actions) and engages your mind so you can effectively think through your strategy.

What I'd like to see in my child:

- Someone who handles money well and is always honest.
- Someone who admits when he forgets to do something and then does it.
- Someone who tells the truth in love, even if it might be hard.
- Someone who can be trusted, because he's straightforward and doesn't lie.

Ideas for getting from here to there:

- Tell him straightforwardly you know he stole the 10 bucks from Grandpa. Ask him why he did it. Tell him that you believe he'll do the right thing, and leave the responsibility in his court for talking to Grandpa and deciding whether he returns the money or not.

- Start an allowance (he's 9—it's about time!) that he gets each week for being part of the family.

- Start a savings account and let him do all the math and accounting.

- If he doesn't feed the dog, don't harp. Without announcing anything, take 50 cents out of his allowance for doing it yourself each time he forgets. Keep an accounting of the times on his pay envelope. He'll figure it out himself after a few weeks.

- Let him experience the consequences of his lies. When he says he isn't feeling well, say, "Oh, that's too bad. I'm making your favorite dessert for dinner. If your brothers and sisters don't finish it off, there might be a smidgen left for you tomorrow, if you're feeling better."

- Let him handle his friendships. But say, "I heard you tell Jake you couldn't play. Is that because you're tired and need time to yourself, or because you're tired of playing with him? Everybody needs time alone by themselves, so you could be honest and tell him that. And if you're tired of playing with him, you need to be kind but honest: 'Jake, I can't play with you every day. I need time by myself and time with other people too.'"

See how it works? Now you try it with the five character traits you'd like to see in your child. Don't worry. I'll still be here when you come back. . . .

Now that you've completed that exercise, congratulations! You've given yourself a road map to get to the destination of the kind of kid—and someday grown-up—you want your child to become. All journeys are undertaken one step or one mile at a time. You don't need to do it all at once. But as you kick off your ideas, here is what you can do for yourself and what you can do for your child.

What you can do for yourself

- Stop guilting or shoulding on yourself. "I should have been a better mother." "I should have been a better father." "If only I'd . . ." "If only I'd not . . ."

Some of what you're facing may be real guilt for things you did do wrong. Or it may be false guilt—owning situations that aren't yours.

What's in the past can't be changed. What you can change, however, is your path from today on. Don't allow the past to tug you backward into guilt, shoulding, and despair. If you do, you will stay mired in the mud and you won't get anywhere.

- Ask a friend, a spouse, or a relative to hold you accountable to following through on your ideas. Have at least a weekly check-in where you can discuss what worked and what didn't and brainstorm with someone who also cares about your child.
- Record your triumphs. They're great milestones not only to rejoice over but to reflect on in your tough moments of parenting.
- Stick to your guns, but don't start or fight the war. Your kid will always win. You back off first, and then they'll back off. If you don't fight, it kinda takes all the fun out of it! Remember that their goal is attention and control. You don't give them either when you step away from a potential fight.

What you can do for your child

- Admit when you blow it. There's nothing sweeter than a true "I'm sorry. I was wrong. Please forgive me" stated in a calm manner to a child who is vying for control. By your simple statement, you take the spark right out of the potential fight.
- Keep those old bones buried. Don't resurrect them from the family yard.
- Don't enable them.

Take yourself out of the position of being the enabler. Don't feel so bad about your child's plight that you let that guilt become the propellant for the decisions you make. Like the woman whose 18-year-old son has already totaled three automobiles. It's amazing the kid still has insurance. He's been kicked up to the highest bracket there is. But guess what his mom wants to do (against his dad's vehement protests)? She wants to buy him a new Mustang with a big engine in it because that's what he really wants. Now let me ask you, who's nuts? The kid or the mom? The kid might be half nuts, but the mom could sell herself to a fruitcake company.

If your son crashes his car or gets his car taken away, don't drive him to work. Let him get his own tail there—whether on a bicycle, with his own two feet, or by bus. Have you ever noticed how many parents line up at school to pick up their kid on a rainy day versus a dry day? Rain doesn't melt your kids' brains. In fact, Gene Kelly did a great job of "Singin' in the Rain," if you ask me.

Or there's the mom who wants to send her son to a heavy-duty university and pay 50 grand a year, but he's smoking dope and drinking and has no respect for her. Again, who's out of whack—the mom or the kid? Both, but the mom started it all.

Many parents today are so overprotective that it's to their kids' detriment.

- Shoot it to them straight, with no wiggle room.

Let's say you have a 15-year-old who is a pain in the keister and won't do a thing around the house. She's sassy with her siblings and expects Mom and Dad to be her slave dogs. In my view, Little Miss Princess needs a dose of reality: "Listen, you've got three more years to be with us in this home. They can be the three best years of your life or hell on earth; it's your choice. But a few basics are going to happen as long as you're living under this roof.

"First, you're going to help out around the house. This is a home, not a hotel or your personal spa. We're all going to work together to help maintain it.

"Second, there are basic rules of mutual respect that we will all adhere to. When they are broken, there will be consequences that neither you nor I will like.

"Third, you will not continue to blow off school as you're doing now. I know what you're capable of doing, but you're underselling yourself. Why you would choose to put yourself down is beyond me.

"To sum it up, how you live your life is your own business. But how you live your life in this home is both your business and mine."

The reality is, your kid wouldn't even have underwear and socks without you. You are her bank, advisor, attorney, primary caregiver, health practitioner, personal limo service, and a whole lot more.

The best place for your child to learn the lessons of life is in the confines of your home, where failure is not only expected (we're all human) but almost encouraged. That's because it is only through failure and mistakes that we learn. A home ought to be a safe place, a place of grace, with a mom and dad who understand that failure is a part of life.

- Act in authority, not as an authoritarian or permissive parent.

I receive a lot of questions from parents about children who seem to be doing okay—well-adjusted kids who do well in school—and then hit a precipice where all of a sudden they get ugly and rebellious, their grades drop, and they run with a different crowd. It seems to happen in the blink of an eye. One of the most common reasons it happens is because there's a parent behind the scenes who has been an authoritarian or permissive parent.

> "How you live your life is your own business. But how you live your life in this home is both your business and mine."

If you're an authoritarian parent, you're strong enough and powerful enough to keep your kids under your thumb for a while. If you're consistently tough, you can control children. The problem comes when they get to that age where they're ready to vote, own or drive a car, drink a beer, or whatever. If they've been brought up with a strictness and control that haven't allowed them to make decisions on their own, they're going to rebel. It's only a matter of when. Think "pastor's daughter."

If you're a permissive parent, you've brought up your child to believe that she always has to be happy, happy, happy at every turn. But that child will rebel too, because there haven't been any rules or guidelines to give her structure.

Too much structure and control lead to rebellion, and so does the "whatever you want—I only want you to be happy" theory of parenting.

The midpoint is authoritative parenting, where you as the parent are the authority in the home. It doesn't make you better than your child—you're both equal in the Creator's eyes—but you play different roles in the home. It means you don't run over your child, and your child doesn't run over you. When a mistake happens, it happens. You grant grace to your child, just as the police officer did to you last Saturday night when he gave you a warning rather than a ticket for not coming to a full stop.

> Too much structure and control lead to rebellion, and so does the "whatever you want—I only want you to be happy" theory of parenting.

Becoming Real

There's a wonderful children's story called *The Velveteen Rabbit* by Margery Williams. It was written in 1922, and it's a classic tale about a splendid toy rabbit given to a child on Christmas morning. As the years go by, the Rabbit is loved so much that he starts to get a little shabby. His friend, the Skin Horse, has lived even longer than the Rabbit and has wisdom to share.

"What is REAL?" asked the Rabbit one day. . . . "Does it mean having things that buzz inside you and a stick-out handle?"

"Real isn't how you are made," said the Skin Horse. "It's a thing that happens to you. When a child loves you for a long, long time, not just to play with, but REALLY loves you, then you become Real."

"Does it hurt?" asked the Rabbit.

"Sometimes," said the Skin Horse, for he was always truthful. "When you are Real you don't mind being hurt."

"Does it happen all at once, like being wound up," he asked, "or bit by bit?"

"It doesn't happen all at once," said the Skin Horse. "You become. It takes a long time. That's why it doesn't happen often to people who break easily, or have sharp edges, or who have to be carefully kept. Generally, by the time you are Real, most of your hair has been loved off, and your eyes drop out and you get loose in the joints and very shabby. But these things don't matter at all, because once you are Real you can't be ugly, except to people who don't understand."[1]

Being real is an essential ingredient to being a good parent. The imperfection of humankind is well established, so who's kidding whom? Yet so many parents come across as know-it-alls—"I've never made a mistake in my life."

Trying to be perfect only incites your power-driven child's need to control—to prove you aren't as perfect as you look and to knock you down a peg or two. But it's hard to be knocked off a pedestal if you're already standing on the floor, isn't it?

> **The imperfection of humankind is well established, so who's kidding whom?**

Being real means that when a kid's performance was rather mediocre, you don't tell them how great they did. You might say, "Hey, a rough day out there today. Things didn't go how you planned." Then you put an arm around the kid, walk them to the car, and say along the way, "You know, we love you—win or lose."

Being real means you tell it like it is with a degree of compassion, but the reality of the situation has to win out. Like the Skin Horse, you have to be honest.

As you are real with your kid and share your human imperfections, your attention-seeking and power-driven child will think, *I remember when Dad got ticked off because he put an X with a permanent black marker on his sock so he'd wear it one more time before he tossed it, and then he put his foot down on the floor in the kitchen. We can still see that X!* Dad was so mad, he told himself how stupid he was and danced around the kitchen growling for a while. Suddenly the stupid things your child has done gain him some perspective. That perfectionistic dad had finally made a boo-boo. *I guess things aren't so bad after all.* And your child actually chuckles, remembering that scene. Perspective and being real halt the drive for power.

So share your failures with your kids. Believe it or not, that power-seeking kid, as much as he may diss you at times, thinks you're perfect and that you walk on water. He can't imagine you doing anything wrong or making mistakes, even though he likes to accuse you of them a lot of the time. So tell your child that you once got in big-time trouble for lying to your parents or you got caught stealing when you were a kid.

My granddaughter Adeline always says, "Grandpa, tell me stories about yourself when you were a little boy."

Sande flashes me that grandma look of "Okay, but you better be selective," since I was really something as a kid.

So I tell Adeline stories. Sometimes I embellish them a little. After all, that's what fathers and grandfathers do. But through those stories, I share morals and teachings with my granddaughter that she will carry through life.

Keep It Simple

Bad habits are hard to break—both yours and your child's. That's why it's important to keep your plan simple:

- Don't ask questions.
- Respond rather than react.
- Keep the long-range goals in mind.

When you change your behavior as a parent, it necessitates that your child will change hers. And that means changing her life mantra too: *I only count when . . .*

Let me tell you about two girls in the National Honor Society. On the outside, both look successful and smart—the kind of kids that firms would like to hire someday.

Myna is the kind of girl who gets attention anywhere she goes. She's determined, flashy, and a natural leader, driven to excel at everything she does. So much so that sometimes she takes shortcuts, like cheating to make the grade. After all, she has to meet the expectations of her perfectionistic business father, who has planned for her to join his company after she graduates from college. But as she walks onstage to be inducted into the National Honor Society, all she can think about is the paper she stole off the internet to finish her science project. *If anybody ever finds out, I'm dead, because my dad's gonna kill me.* And then her chin firms up, because she has her own plans, and they don't include ever working with her dad.

Addie has worked hard to get into the National Honor Society, because she's a determined child. She comes from a family with a powerful work ethic, and she knows that being in the National Honor Society will help her get into the college of her choice. But academics aren't the only things that make her tick. She's developed a heart for the homeless, and for the past four years she, her little brother, and her parents have packed up a big bag of homemade sandwiches every Saturday and handed them out at a nearby park.

They provide not only food but clothing and counseling. Her father recently helped one man, an accountant who had fallen on hard times, find a job. When her parents look at Addie walking across the stage to be inducted into the society, tears of joy flow. She was not only the kind of kid they'd wanted when they held that little 20-incher in their arms, but she'd gone far beyond their dreams. She is smart and hardworking, and above all, she cares about others.

Both girls are powerful children. Five years earlier, Addie's parents went through a rough period with her where she constantly argued with them and fought with her brother. But with calmness and patience, they'd worked through it as a family. In fact, that rough period had launched their sandwich ministry, and they'd all grown to love it. With her parents' help, Addie had turned her attention-seeking, power-driven behavior into skills that could help others.

So what kind of kid do you want?

Back to our pie analogy. On the outside, both girls appear to be browned perfectly; the crusts are flaky and appetizing. But inside, the ingredients are completely different. Myna's is made with ingredients you'd never want to put into a pie. Addie's is made with finely mixed ingredients.

But the proof of the ingredients is in that first bite of pie. There's either a satisfied "Ahh . . ." from those around them, complete with a big smile at the tantalizing flavor, or there's a shocked, dismayed "What the heck is in this pie?" response.

Are you raising a self-absorbed child who thinks she's the best thing since sliced bread? Are you giving her real-life tools she can use, or just allowing yourself to be dragged along for the ride?

What you put into your kid's pie makes all the difference in the fragrance she will make down the road.

Will she be a mud pie, or a fragrant, homegrown, melt-in-your-mouth kind of pie?

The choice, parent, is up to you while that child is still in your home.

After that, the choice is up to your child.

Powerful Ideas That Work

My son, Peter, was 7 when he flattened another boy on the playground who had tried to add the top ball to his snowman. At 9, he was sent home from a school field trip because he pushed another kid into a pond when they were touring a garden. At 13, he decked that same kid—knocked him out cold—when he made a comment about Peter being black.

I've made more trips to the school office than I care to say. Peter is a very physical kind of kid, and he tends to react quickly if he thinks he's being wronged. I was that way as a kid too, so I get it. But I'd never told him that.

I took him for a father-son weekend to a cabin a friend let us use for free, and we grilled hot dogs, roasted marshmallows, and had snowball fights. We also sat around the fire a lot and talked. I told him about the trouble I got into as a kid, and he told me how frustrated he got with the kid at school who called him names because he's black. I told him about my own experiences growing up as "poor white trash." I talked about the times I handled things badly and then how good it felt when I realized how insecure those other guys were, and that when I fought back, I gave them exactly what they wanted. I could tell the lightbulb went on.

The two months since then have been fistfight-free. Peter told me the kid at school tried to get him mad, but he just shrugged. He heard the kid walk off and say, "Well, that didn't work"—out loud. We laughed about it. It's sure good to hear laughs instead of yelling in our house now.

Lambert, Oregon

Power Points

- Start with the end in mind.
- Stick with the plan.
- Be real.
- Keep it simple.

14

Grace-Based Parenting

For the prodigal in your life.

Have you ever watched a dog hunting for a bone he buried in the backyard? That critter is relentless in his search, sniffing around, leaving no stone unturned until he finds that bone. And then he does something surprising. He looks in all directions to make sure no one has seen his prize and then buries it again! It makes me scratch my head, although it's typical doggie behavior. Why would somebody bury a bone only to dig it up and then bury it again—and do this not only once but multiple times?

Dogs are so like humans sometimes, aren't they?

You'll find bone-digging adults in every generation and in both sexes. These are the people who seem to remember every violation of the family rules that your son or daughter has committed over their entire presence on this earth. We could all take a tip from my friend Tim Kimmel's great book called *Grace-Based Parenting*. Grace and forgiveness are wonderful things. When your kids mess up, they need your grace. They need your forgiveness. When they've received both, it's your responsibility to bury that bone—permanently. You can't be like the dog that goes out in the backyard and starts digging for that scruffy old bone.

> **Bone-digging is a relationship killer, like spraying Raid on a cockroach from two inches away.**

Yet not only do some parents dig up that bone once, but they dig it up over and over, beating the poor kid over the noodle with that same scruffy bone. If you want to permanently shut down conversation with your kids, continue bone-digging. Do it long enough and you'll end the relationship. Bone-digging is a relationship killer, like spraying Raid on a cockroach from two inches away.

If you're a person of faith, there is additional motivation. Let me be frank. God says if you don't forgive others, then guess what? He's not forgiving you.[2] Powerful words.

Never are the elements of grace and forgiveness more important than with a powerful child who becomes a prodigal.

What Would You Do If . . . ?

You get a call from Mr. Murphey, the assistant principal of the middle school. He wants you to come in and talk about an incident that happened today that involved your daughter, Samantha.

"What's this about?" you manage.

"We'd probably best talk about this face-to-face," he responds. "I'd like to talk with you first, and then with you *and* your daughter, if that's okay."

You show up at school, and Mr. Murphey greets you warmly. But you have a gut feeling you aren't going to like what you're about to hear.

He hands you a note that your daughter wrote, which was passed along to two girls about another girl. In the note, Samantha calls the girl names you don't want to mention and threatens that the girl will regret it the rest of her life if she even tries to talk to your daughter.

(By the way, sadly, this is very characteristic of kids in middle school, and particularly girls. Girls are nasty with their words. Boys tend to get into fistfights to prove their power and dominance; girls fight for power and dominance with their words.)

Your jaw drops. This goes way beyond the catty "I don't like her" scenario. You have no idea where your daughter even learned these words. You don't use them at home, and you don't know anybody who uses them. You're completely stunned.

> **Boys tend to get into fistfights to prove their power and dominance; girls fight for power and dominance with their words.**

Then your daughter is ushered into the office. The look on her face says, "Uh-oh."

Mr. Murphey says, "Mrs. Clark, would you read this note that your daughter has offered?"

You start reading it aloud and burst into tears.

"Listen, you're having a hard time with that," Mr. Murphey says calmly. "Samantha, why don't you read it?"

Samantha manages to choke out the words.

The assistant principal—by now, in spite of your embarrassment, you've pegged him as a really smart guy—says, "Sam, is this note reflective of who you are?"

She can't answer.

Finally, the meeting is over.

Result #1

You and your daughter are stone silent the entire car ride home. You are so furious and embarrassed that you're shaking. She is so embarrassed and scared that she turns her head away from you and toward the window so you can't see the tears glimmering in her eyes.

As soon as you get home, you hammer the nail in her coffin. "Young lady, how dare you write a note like that. You are grounded for a month. No, make that two months. And don't push me or it'll be even longer."

Conversation is cut off completely, and both of you go away angry.

Result #2

Your daughter is quiet in the car, and so are you. When you get home, she faces you with some tears, an apology, and a lot of guilt. That's because she realizes that her mother has just seen who she really is.

But is that who your child is, really?

If you're smart, you'll take the apology, smooth the tears, and put some time between that event and what you'll need to talk about with her later. That's because this needs to be a teachable moment, where your powerful child, who is obviously a ringleader and powerful among girls, needs to understand that what she does affects what others think of her.

A couple hours later you sit down with your daughter and have a little chat. It can go something like this:

"Mr. Murphey brought up a good question, Sam. Is this note an indication of who you are? All through life, people will make judgments about you based on what you say and do. But there will come a time, in about six years, where a university admissions officer is going to look at a single eight-by-eleven piece of paper or a computer screen and make all kinds of judgments about who Samantha Clark is. That's why it's important that your words match your actions."

If you're part of a Christian family, you might even want to add, "Philippians 4:8 says to think about whatever is good, honorable, right, and true."

Then you go on. "Honey, we all make mistakes. We say things we shouldn't say. Let me tell you about what happened to me growing up . . ."

And you share about the mean things that happened to you and to others—things that pitted kids against each other. You note that they were spawned out of immaturity, selfishness, and a fear of not being the top in the pecking order. "You never knew who would be next in the peer group to be picked on. You just hoped it wouldn't be you. You need to understand that as your parent, I've made a lot of bad decisions in life too."

Next you slip her what I call "the commercial announcement."

"I know you, Sam, and I know that the note you passed is not reflective of who you really are. I know you have a kind heart, because I've seen your kindness many times. But I'm always going to expect the best of you. I know that doing the best thing and doing the right thing aren't always easy. You're going to be surrounded by people who will try to influence you to do the wrong thing.

"Let's consider this negative page closed. We're going to wipe the slate clean. You are our daughter, and you will always have our support. We will always have positive expectations for you."

What are you offering here as a parent? A positive, forward-thinking statement that says, "I'm not going to be a bone-digger here. I won't bang you over the head with the incident. God says not to judge others, so I won't judge you. Know that you're loved, we believe in you, and life will go on."

By doing this, you have diffused the power surge that would otherwise come if she felt that you, her parent, was against her and was going to hammer her.

Once again, you are that circuit breaker.

Stop. Look. Listen.

Years ago, before the old railroad tracks had those blinkers, there was a simple sign that said, "Stop. Look. Listen." Train horns were blown before a train came to the intersection. That meant if you were driving your car or walking, you had to stop, look around, and listen.

In the situation with your prodigal, *stop* means that you evaluate what you would normally do—before you do it. What would the old you do in this situation?

Look means that you take a careful look at what the new you is going to do differently—and then you do it.

Listen means that you listen with calmness and a compassionate heart to what your child may be thinking or feeling. But you also don't let it sway your next steps. You let the situation play out.

What you can do

- Never own what isn't yours. Don't take on the responsibility that your prodigal ought to be taking on herself. Teachable moments aren't nearly as teachable if the sting of consequences doesn't accompany them.

- Don't assume anything. Even the "facts" can be interpreted differently by different parties. Listen to the facts from all sides, and then ask almighty God for discernment.

Now, back to Sam, our prodigal. After you talked with her, you reconnected the next day with Mr. Murphey. He assured you that he was going to gather the girls who were passing the note, including Sam, in his office to find out what was going on. And he was certainly going to remind them of how to treat people—the way they'd like to be treated. You also asked

> **Don't take on the responsibility that your prodigal ought to be taking on herself.**

him to keep in touch with you about your daughter: "I'd like to see what's going on with her in the classroom, and to see if your and my conversations with her have made an impact."

Imagine your surprise when Mr. Murphey calls two weeks later. This time it's a call that affirms Sam is the kind of girl you thought she was. When a new girl transferred in—an outsider who wasn't the typical Anglo kid in the classroom and could have a difficult time fitting in—Sam was the one who chose to sit with her at lunch. She also introduced her to other kids at the school.

You sigh with relief. Your prodigal might be back on the right track.

Hanging Tough

At a seminar in Texas one evening, Sarah, an elementary school principal, shared with me that a third grader at her school had been suspended three times because she was hitting kids and calling them names.

I said, "Isn't some kid gonna clean her clock someday?"

Sarah sighed. "They're all afraid of her."

"Well," I replied, getting into psychologist mode, "what does the parent do?"

She exhaled. "Nothing. The mom tells me she grounded her."

I rolled my eyes.

Sarah went on to tell me that she'd found an excuse to drop something off at the mom's house, to see if she was really following through on discipline, and the mom came up with all sorts of excuses. She said that the in-house suspension was just too rough on their family.

"Where is she now?" Sarah asked the girl's mother.

The mother hedged. "Uh, she took off."

Duh. Go get her; you're the parent, Sarah couldn't help but think. But at that point, she realized the girl would continue her power-driven behavior because there were no guidelines, no one to stop her.

That kid had already seen 16 or 17 "experts" to help resolve the situation. That's because the mother wanted her to get "fixed" without doing anything herself. And the solution was right in her own home.

Excuses only make the weak weaker. And a kid who is power-driven is already weak, because she sees herself as only important when she rules. Her life mantra is, *I only count when I'm in charge.* That third grader is actually very insecure.

> **Excuses only make the weak weaker.**

Very powerful people don't like it when others are powerful toward them, but they do respect it.

The best thing you can do for your prodigal is to put the ball in their court and hang tough.

Reality-Based Parenting

I love the story of the prodigal son in the Bible. That powerful kid wanted his own way and control over his life. So he went to his father and demanded his just due. His father could have said, "I'm not giving you a dime." Instead, he was overly generous.

The kid took his entire inheritance and headed for a faraway land—as far as he could go from his home, which felt like a jail to him. He didn't want any more attachments to family. He was sick and tired of them. They were always telling him what to do, to be more responsible like his brother. He only wanted to have fun.

So that was exactly what he decided to do—have fun . . . until the money ran out. Then he discovered his friends weren't exactly what he thought they were. He began thinking about that jail cell called home, which no longer looked like imprisonment. In fact, it looked pretty good compared to where he was living now.

But the kid had to hit rock bottom before he could make steps forward. He had to figure out that his father's farmhands were better off than he was.

His father was a smart dad. He didn't pursue his son. He knew his son would only have run harder and faster to get away from him. Instead, he did the hard thing. He waited, and waited, and waited. He kept the light on and the door open, hoping and praying for his son's return.

That reality-based parenting is why I tell parents of prodigals, "When your prodigal takes off, don't send her money or even a birthday card. You usually don't have an address to send a card to anyway. Any efforts will only say to them that you're seeking to control their lives, and your powerful kid will run faster and harder. So you do the hard thing. You sit and do nothing. But you do pray for your kid. Especially since the instant she decides that she knows more than you do and wants to live life on her own terms, without regard for anyone else, she's at risk. Once she leaves the comfort and safety of your home, she's at risk. Bad things can happen to her. Kids who flee to the streets pay for it in ways they'd never have imagined.

"But you also do what the father of that prodigal did—you leave the lights on and the door open."

Spending time going over and over what you did wrong with your child won't gain you anything—other than guilt, stress, and a heart condition.

What's in the past is in the past.

What's in the past is in the past, and it should stay buried, like that bone in your yard. You could have been a nearly perfect parent and still have had a powerful child who went the way of a prodigal.

Nothing in life, or in parenting, is guaranteed, except for the grace and forgiveness of the Almighty.

The same grace and forgiveness you need to offer your prodigal.

Powerful Ideas That Work

Our daughter, Jane, was 16 years old when she took off. She left us a note, saying she was sick of the rules and that we needed to "wake up and join the real world." We'd known she was unhappy but had no idea she was that unhappy. We'd figured her moodiness and silence was just a teenage thing. We hadn't faced anything like it with our son, who is four years older, so we were unprepared. My wife sobbed for days. Both of us talked about the way we'd raised her and wondered what we'd done wrong.

We didn't hear from her for three years. At times we thought she might be dead, but we hung on to hope. Hearing you talk about powerful children took the edge off our grief, and we began to realize what things in her childhood we could have done differently and also what things we had no control over. As you said, "Don't own what isn't yours."

Three years ago, Jane called. She sounded different—quieter somehow. There wasn't the usual sassiness. She hung up quickly before we could ask any questions about where she was. So we waited more and prayed. Two months after that, she called again and asked for our forgiveness. She said she wanted to come home. That someone else needed us too. We figured she was bringing a boyfriend home.

We arranged for two bus tickets home and met her—and our 9-month-old grandson—at the station with open arms. Now we're a family again, plus one. And this year, with our help, Jane will return to school to get her GED. Thank you, Dr. Leman, for providing perspective when we needed it most.

Richard, North Carolina

Power Points

- Don't be a bone-digger.
- Don't own what isn't yours.
- Hang tough and pray.
- Extend forgiveness and grace.

15

Rewiring Your Home

*What you used to say, and what you'll say now
that you know all of your child's strategies.*

It's time to do a little check. How does a typical day at your home begin? What are the words you choose to say to your son or daughter first thing in the morning? Are they commands? Questions? Do they sound anything like one of these?

- "Are you deaf or something? Don't you hear me? You've got to get up. I can hear the bus. It's in the neighborhood."
- "I'm telling you for the very last time. You know, I've about had it with you."
- "Hello! Your pancakes are turning into ice cubes. Don't be complaining to me that they're cold."
- "Your alarm clock's gone off five times."
- "All right, I'm going to get a bucket of water."
- "Do you have your clarinet? It's band day."

- "You can't wear that. It's 37 degrees out. Go and change."
- "If you think you're going to school like that, young man, you're wrong. Whatever you did to your hair, undo it."
- "Listen, if you think you're wearing that skeleton earring, you're not. If you have to wear it with your guy friends on the weekend, I guess I'll let it pass. But you're not wearing it to school."
- "How many times do I have to tell you, mind your own business. Your sister can make that decision by herself. She doesn't need you."
- "Keep your hands to yourself."
- "You wanna go to your room?"
- "If a bird had your brain, he'd fly sideways."
- "You're going to be the death of me yet."
- "You drive me completely insane."
- "All right, but this is the last time I'm driving you to school."
- "No, you're not taking three Snickers bars for lunch. You're gonna get worms and lose all your teeth. Then I'll have to take you to the vet and deworm you."
- "I can't wait until your father gets home, because I'm going to remember this moment, and he's going to hear every word you just said. I wouldn't want to be in your shoes tonight."
- "I've got a mind not to let you go to prom."

And then a few that fathers are famous for:

- "Don't talk to your mother like that."
- "Why's the front door open? What are we doing, heating the neighborhood?"
- "Do you think money grows on trees?"

- "Get that look off your face right now, or I'll change it for you."
- "That garbage is still sitting there. It doesn't take itself out, you know. Hello, it's Monday."
- "You two deserve each other." (Said to warring siblings.)
- "Why we had children, I'll never know. Chinchillas. We shoulda had chinchillas."

And with these comments—usually launched by you—the volleyball game begins bright and early. If you don't start the conversation, then you tend to up the ante when you volley back.

In for the Kill?

Volleyball is a great sport. If you've ever had the occasion to watch college volleyball or skilled high school volleyball, it's fascinating. The ball is launched over the net, and a setter sets the ball straight up in the air so that the big, tall spiker can smash it to the floor, earning that team a point. That's called a kill.

It's a little like what parents do, but they often play both the setter and the spiker. They set up the kid to fight, and then they spout a comment that's like a kill—a slam dunk to the floor.

It usually ends with something like, "And that's FINAL!" You would have thought that Julius Caesar himself in his toga walked into the room and pronounced judgment on the scene.

What happens next?

If there's one thing that can get a parent going, it's when they issue a dictate or command and their powerful kid gives them the "I couldn't care less" look. It's fuel for the fire in your belly, isn't it? Admit it.

If you're like most parents, you'll fire back—put the kid in his place.

But ask yourself, is that really what you want to do?

This chapter is called "Rewiring Your Home." You're the master electrician here. You know the difference between the red wire and the black wire and what sparks a fight. You can feel it coming—whether it's a fight between siblings or between yourself and your power-driven child.

> **You would have thought that Julius Caesar himself in his toga walked into the room and pronounced judgment on the scene.**

Remember, though, that you're the adult here (see chapter 12). A child doesn't get power out of thin air. He learns to be powerful by interacting with powerful people. It's possible the other powerful person is a sibling, but in all probability it's one (or both) of the parents—the one issuing all those authoritarian orders at the beginning of this chapter.

But the good news is that if you've learned that powerful, authoritarian way of barking out orders, you can unlearn it and then do something different.

In fact, it's as simple as ABC:

- Action on your part
- Behavior modification and control on your part
- Change completed!

Take Two

Let's replay the scenes above with you focusing on that ABC. What did you use to say, and what will you say and do now that's different?

216

Scenario #1

What you used to say: "Are you deaf or something? Don't you hear me? You've got to get up. I can hear the bus. It's in the neighborhood."

What you'll say and do now: "Joshua, you might want to know that it's 8:20." You say it once, then turn your back and walk away.

Don't even go there with the pestering. This new statement is milder, and it's not apt to set off the trigger in your power-driven child. Most power-driven kids are going to find a way to be negative with whatever you say to them. But you don't want to incite their fury by rubbing their nose in it. And that's what parents tend to do—play the one-upmanship game. In effect, you're saying, "I'm bigger than you are, so you have to do what I ask you to do." Nothing kicks off a fight more than a superior attitude.

Scenario #2

What you used to say: "I'm telling you for the very last time. You know, I've about had it with you."

What you'll say and do now: Nothing. Don't tell him for the last time, because you already told him. Say it once, and let that be a teachable moment. Never repeat yourself. Where is it written in the parental guidebook that you have to remind your child? Think of reminders this way: they are actually disrespectful acts. So are warnings. The respectful

> **Nothing kicks off a fight more than a superior attitude.**

thing to do is to hold your child accountable for what he does in life.

Did you learn from your mistakes growing up? Do you learn from your mistakes as an adult? What makes you think your son or daughter isn't going to learn from their mistakes? Your rewired home needs to be a place where failure isn't fatal. There has to be an atmosphere of grace.

Scenario #3

What you used to say: "Hello! Your pancakes are turning into ice cubes. Don't be complaining to me that they're cold."

What you'll say and do now: Twelve minutes later, your child finally comes to breakfast and says, "Hey, my pancakes are cold!" You say, "Well, I've gotta tell you the truth—mine were warm and tasty 12 minutes ago." It's a way of slipping your kid a commercial announcement. (It's better than what you want to say: "Hey, stupid, if you would have been here 12 minutes ago, you and I would have enjoyed warm, tasty pancakes together, and we could have bonded.") Or you could be even more straightforward and say, "I bet they are. Could it have anything to do with the fact that when I called you and the pancakes were warm and fresh off the griddle, you chose to hit the snooze alarm in your head and get some extra minutes of sleep?"

Don't look for trouble.

Don't look for trouble. As I love to say, "Keep your sails out of your child's wind."

Every parent on the planet vows at one point, "I'm never going to say that to my kid in the same tone my parents said it to me." Don't kid yourself. You're a creature of habit. We're all emotional creatures of habit. We tend to say to our kids what our parents said to us. Take a look at the research on kids who were abused. You don't need a master's degree to figure out the result, do you? Kids who are abused grow into adults who abuse their children. If a kid lives with criticism, he'll grow up to criticize other people too.

Scenario #4

What you used to say: "Your alarm clock's gone off five times."
"All right, I'm going to get a bucket of water."

What you'll say and do now: Shut your mouth, walk away, and understand that your child will be late today. It will be an inconvenience for you as a parent, but just having children is a huge inconvenience. So you might as well put a seat belt on and enjoy the ride. Sometimes being a good parent means shutting your mouth and letting life unfurl. It means letting your son or daughter experience the consequences of their poor decisions.

Scenario #5

What you used to say: "Do you have your clarinet? It's band day."

What you'll say and do now: Is it your clarinet? Then why should you say or do anything? Okay, I know you rent the clarinet, but it's your child's. Don't own what isn't yours. When you step into ownership, you weaken your powerful child's ability to make healthy decisions. This is one of those times where you need to shut up, even when you're tempted to do otherwise.

Scenario #6

What you used to say: "You can't wear that. It's 37 degrees out. Go and change."

"If you think you're going to school like that, young man, you're wrong. Whatever you did to your hair, undo it."

"Listen, if you think you're wearing that skeleton earring, you're not. If you have to wear it with your guy friends on the weekend, I guess I'll let it pass. But you're not wearing it to school."

What you'll say and do now: As hard as it is not to see yourself as a fashion designer, think back to all the dumb things you wore as a kid. Every generation has their own style of dressing. My generation had draped pants that were tight at the ankles and baggy the rest of the way up. If they were royal blue, so much the better. And the greasier the hair, the better. If you could get a little curl going on your forehead and look like the late Tony Curtis, you were awesome.

Stupid looking, but awesome.

Aren't you glad we have pictures to remind ourselves of what we were like in our day?

Every generation goes out of its way to be sure they are different from the one before them (their parents' generation). It happens the world over, friends, but deal with it in as positive a way as you possibly can.

> **Every generation goes out of its way to be sure they are different from the one before them.**

However, with that said, if the outfit doesn't fit the season at all, you have every right to say, "I see you're not ready to go to school yet. I happened to notice that it's 37 degrees out and you have shorts on." This works best in a situation where you're driving your child to school. It's also especially important if your child has a low immunity.

Your child will give you the "Oh, come on, or we'll be late" line. And you say calmly, "I'll take you when you're ready."

Sometimes you have to play that card. Other times you don't, and your kid freezes her tail off. And when she does, she might think, *Huh, maybe this would have been a good day to wear long pants.*

Ah, lesson learned . . . and without your harping.

Scenario #7

What you used to say: "How many times do I have to tell you, mind your own business. Your sister can make that decision by herself. She doesn't need you."

"Keep your hands to yourself."

What you'll say and do now: Let the siblings work it out between them. If you stay out of the fight—and, even better, remove yourself from the room—it's amazing how swiftly a fight can fizzle out. That's because your two powerful, attention-seeking kids no longer have an audience.

> **"Row your own canoe."**

I used to tell my kids, "Row your own canoe" anytime they decided to get into a fracas with each other. It usually ended the argument quickly.

Scenario #8

What you used to say: "If a bird had your brain, he'd fly sideways."

"You're going to be the death of me yet."

"You drive me completely insane."

What you'll say and do now: An apology is due. You went way over the line and made a fool of yourself. You have a responsibility to say the redemptive words, "I'm sorry. I shouldn't have said that. Please forgive me for my thoughtlessness." Believe it or not, those words knock down barriers, opening hearts and minds. Words are very personal. They either move right to the jugular vein or soothe a wounded heart, so consider them carefully before you say them.

Scenario #9

What you used to say: "All right, but this is the last time I've driving you to school."

What you'll say and do now: In all probability, this isn't the last time, because you've already taught your son or daughter that what you say really doesn't mean anything. The fact that you repeat things further proves it. So again, who is the organ grinder and who is the monkey? Who's training whom?

We train our kids not to listen to us, to blow off whatever we say. That's because they live with us and know that we might huff and puff, but by the end of the day we'll get over it, and then the kids are free to go to the game they want to go to.

If you use the "this is the last time" language, your kids end up anesthetized. Ditto for the word *no* with toddlers. They're so hammered with it by the time they're 4 years old that it has lost its meaning. So say "no" less. Instead,

> **We train our kids not to listen to us, to blow off whatever we say.**

pick up your toddler and divert his attention from whatever he's doing that you don't want him to. Remove him to another part of the home. That's teaching and training the child but doing it in an action-oriented way. Then the needless barbs and cheap shots that parents can be so good at with their kids won't be necessary. "No" will be used only when it really counts. Then your powerful kid will know you mean business.

Scenario #10

What you used to say: "No, you're not taking three Snickers bars for lunch. You're gonna get worms and lose all your teeth. Then I'll have to take you to the vet and deworm you."

What you'll say and do now: Since you care about what your child eats, and you've read a lot of articles about the health and nutrition of children, you take the three Snickers bars out of her lunch. You say gently, "Honey, I know it's tempting, but we'll leave these for another time." Part of good parenting is remaining in control of your emotions—not overdoing things, being pragmatic and action-oriented, and thinking your way to behavioral change.

Scenario #11

What you used to say: "I can't wait until your father gets home, because I'm going to remember this moment, and he's going to hear every word you just said. I wouldn't want to be in your shoes tonight."

"I've got a mind not to let you go to prom."

"Don't talk to your mother like that."

What you'll say and do now: Kids see through threats and warnings very quickly. The more repetitive they are, the less meaning they'll have. Every word you say, you're accountable for. People say "you make me mad" all the time, but the reality is, you choose to be mad. You're the one who makes the decision to blurt out words that hurt.

If you walk into a room that your kids have destroyed—one you recently picked up—a good, healthy thing to say is, "I am so angry and upset at the sight of this room." Notice that this is an honest statement. You are angry, and you are upset. You're showing your displeasure that your kids have chosen to diss the room you cleaned. But you also spoke the truth in love. You say it once, and then you walk away.

Here's an important principle you need to know: by saying you're angry and upset, you've raked hot coals over your kids, because they don't like it when Mom or Dad is upset. Few parents understand that, but it's a great form of discipline. If your kids have even a shred of morality or decency, they'll quickly go in and take care of that room they messed up.

Speaking the truth in love and with a calm voice goes a long way in dealing with discipline issues. Passing the buck—"I can't wait until your father gets home"—is a sign of weakness. If something happens on your watch, *you* deal with it. Don't put your mate in that precarious position of walking into a situation they didn't witness and didn't experience and then being thrust into the role of Judge Judy. Not only is that unfair, but it does you both a disservice and weakens your parental authority.

> **You say it once, and then you walk away.**

Scenario #12

What you used to say: "Why's the front door open? What are we doing, heating the neighborhood?"

"Do you think money grows on trees?"

What you'll say and do now: Realize that what you're saying is a put-down. Instead, say, "Katherine, would you please close the front door? I see someone left it open." In all probability, if Katherine was the culprit, she'll say, "Sorry, Dad." At least that's what most kids—even power-driven ones—will say if approached that way. It focuses on the *action* instead of the *actor* in those situations. If you try to rub a kid's nose in their mistake, it won't help your relationship at all. It sets your kid against you.

Scenario #13

What you used to say: "Get that look off your face right now, or I'll change it for you."

What you'll say and do now: You might say, "I can see by the look on your face that you're not happy with what I asked you to do." That statement opens the door for some discussion rather than leading to hurling insults at each other. It shows that you respect your child's opinion and thoughts, and it allows you a teachable moment: "There are a few things we ask you to do every day and every week in this home, and we do that for a reason. You are a member of this family, and you benefit from all the amenities this family offers."

Scenario #14

What you used to say: "That garbage is still sitting there. It doesn't take itself out, you know. Hello, it's Monday."

"You two deserve each other." (Said to warring siblings.)

"Why we had children, I'll never know. Chinchillas. We shoulda had chinchillas."

What you'll say and do now: An apology is due. You're dissing your kids.

Okay, now you try it:

Scenario #15

What you used to say:

What you'll say and do now:

Scenario #16

What you used to say:

What you'll say and do now:

Look at you—you're getting to be an expert already!

Back to Those Goals of Misbehavior

Remember the four goals of misbehavior from chapter 9? Your feelings, parent, are a good clue that will point you to your child's mistaken goal. But if you come up with a positive response—instead of thinking, *I'm going to punish this kid for what he just did*—you short-circuit the goal of attention or power. Punishment doesn't teach a kid anything. Discipline teaches him how to be a contributing member to your family and society.

In his article "The Four Mistaken Goals of Children's Misbehaviour," psychologist Larry Nisan did a great job of adapting concepts from Rudolf Dreikurs's book *Children: The Challenge*, and so with thanks, I adapt these ideas from Larry.

Seeking Undue Attention

What your child's behavior is saying: *I only count in this world when I keep you busy with me.*

Your gut emotional response: *You are so annoying. What a pain in the neck!*

What you do as a result: You ignore the behavior.

How your child reacts to your mistaken responses and measures: He ramps up the behavior.

What you should do instead: Give your child due attention (i.e., encouragement, not praise) when it is not being sought.

Seeking Undue Power

What your child's behavior is saying: *I only count in this world when I show you I am boss or when I make you do something.* Or: *I only count in this world when I show you that you can't make me do anything.*

Your gut emotional response:

- Angry: *This kid really ticks me off.*
- Challenged: *I'd like to rub his nose in it.*
- Frustrated: *If I could UPS her someplace, I would.*
- Defeated: *Sheesh, this is impossible; there's no way out.*
- Retaliatory: *I'll show you who's boss, you little rat.*
- Increased intensity: *I'm going to make you miserable for pulling this power play on me.*

What you do as a result: You intensify the power play on your end and up the ante.

How your child reacts to your mistaken responses and measures: He ramps up the power play.

What you should do instead:

- Listen first.
- Always offer a choice.
- Negotiate reasonable limits of time and action.[3]

Here's how it works.

"You hate me," your kid says.

Most parents would say, "Now, honey, why would you say that?" and they get all shocked, offended, and in a huff.

A good response would be, "If you want to believe that, you go right ahead. I know it's not true."

Why is this a good response? Because you're acknowledging the power of your kid ("I know you're a strong-willed person"), and you're acknowledging his feelings ("I understand you're upset. You're angry. I get that. But this is the way it is").

Feelings are feelings; you can't deny or manipulate them. So give your child permission to feel the way he does, then speak the truth in love.

I guarantee your power-driven, attention-seeking kid will change if you're willing to put time and effort into changing yourself. So ask yourself what you normally would do in a powerful situation with your son or daughter. Then ask yourself, *What am I going to do and say differently?* Change is all about making the choice to behave differently.

What you can do

- Realize your child's goals.
- Master your child's trigger points so you don't set them into motion.
- Acknowledge your child's feelings, then speak the truth in love.

Rewiring Your Own Behavior

Just as you're trying to rewire your powerful kid's behavior, you're also rewiring yours. What happens between you and your child now will continue to spark if you don't do something different.

Does your 4-year-old always get in fights with his 6-year-old sister? Is this the scenario: he cries, you run to his aid, and you admonish his sister?

That gives your attention-seeking, power-driven 4-year-old exactly what he wants. So what are you going to do differently to halt his behavior?

What you can do

- Disengage from the battle.

The next time he runs to you, crying about something his sister said or did, you say, "Honey, you have a problem with your sister. You need to talk to your sister about it." Then you turn and walk out of the room. The two will be forced to work out the issue if you aren't there to play referee.

If you don't act, your 4-year-old is going to become one of those adults who complains about another employee in the break room and then runs to his boss to tattle. A healthy adult learns to work out his own relational struggles. Unhealthy adults find it easier to complain.

> **Change is all about making the choice to behave differently.**

Then, when confronted, they backpedal quickly because at their core, they are insecure.

When you rewire your own behavior, you change the expected outcome. If you disengage from sibling warfare, you're acknowledging that it's their battle, not yours. Most kids will continue to whine if they've learned that when they whine, they get their six-foot-two dad to intercede for them with their four-foot-seven brother.

Remember that you're the original power source. It's not that you have all of life's answers in your back pocket—your kids will see through that idea in a minute. But a soft answer goes a long way: "Honey, I may be wrong, but could it be that one of the ways you make sure you feel good about yourself is by putting your sister down? Isn't there a better way of dealing with that? Aren't there some things you could say about yourself right now that are very positive? Like the fact that you do well in school and you're working hard to learn the rules of soccer? So why are you working so hard to compare yourself to your sister?"

> **When you rewire your own behavior, you change the expected outcome.**

- Get to know your own hot buttons.

"Dr. Leman, I'm pretty calm most of the time," a mom told me recently. "But then my kid continues to push my buttons and I explode." Welcome to the 99 percent of humanity club. There are certain statements and behaviors that trigger your temper. But does that mean you have to explode?

You be the parent here. Find a way of neutralizing your reactions. Think through how you'll respond *before* those heated situations happen. If you have a well-thought-out plan for the common actions and reactions in your home, you'll be looking for the opportunity to carry it out, not surprised when those events happen to heat up the temperature in your home. Is it that eye roll? Her "No way"? The crossed-arm body posture? Or the "But Mom . . ." that starts the litany of offenses you've carried out against her?

Come up with strategies now, before those actions and words kick off.

- Realize some things are worth going to war over and some aren't.

When your power-driven kid says something stupid—and don't worry, he will—your response will have everything to do with what happens next. So instead of saying, "That's the dumbest thing I've ever heard," swallow that knee-jerk reaction. Look him straight in the eye and say, "Tell me more about that."

Teeter-Totter Philosophy

Remember when you sat on a teeter-totter as a kid? We already talked about you, the parent, being the middle balance point on that teeter-totter. But think about the principle of a teeter-totter for a minute. It's a one-to-one relationship where one of you goes up when the other goes down. It's the same with power in a relationship. If person A becomes powerful, then tries to push person B down and succeeds, person A's power level increases. And the instinctual reaction of person B, who is being forced down, is to do what kids in my neighborhood loved to do: wait until a critical moment and then jump off the teeter-totter, sending the other kid crashing to earth.

But what if you put your feet on the ground on your end of that teeter-totter and tried to even out the motion instead?

Either way, you're acting, but one action has negative results (the other person goes down hard on their bum and you get yelled at), and the other has positive, calming results (you both have a minute to enjoy the blue sky above you).

For example, let's say your powerful kid stomps in the back door and slams her books on the kitchen table. She spouts, "I've absolutely had it with Jessica."

You know she and Jessica have been friends for three years and have had their ups and downs. Most parents would jump right in and say, "Oh, honey, what's wrong?" But you'd be smart to let your kid unwind a little. Letting her stomp off to her room for some alone time will do her—and you—good. Sooner or later you'll find out what's wrong anyway, after she's had time to process.

If you pry and ask questions, even though it's obvious she's upset, be ready for "You'd never understand" and "Why are you so nosy?" So any response sets you up for a fight, because your daughter is raring for a fight with someone. If you're in the kitchen, you're an easy pick.

The reality is, your daughter is most likely hurting if she's that angry. She might really need your help.

But not right now. Not until she's cooled off will she even be able to talk rationally or to hear anything you might wish to say.

However, if you start grilling her like an attorney, firing questions at her, her mouth will zip shut and her power-driven behavior will rear its head.

If you keep your cool, you'll be amazed what you find out. She'll have a need to tell you because you're not pushing.

It's a law of physics: if there's movement one way, there has to be movement another way.

If you power down, your child has no reason to power up.

Powerful Ideas That Work

My 11-year-old son likes to get in his 13-year-old stepsister's face. She doesn't back down either. Since my wife and I married two years ago, it's been like World War III. The only time it's quiet in our house is after two doors slam and both kids sulk in their rooms for at least an hour.

Then my wife heard you on the radio, talking about birth order and how to handle sibling rivalry. For the first time, we realized that we had two firstborns jockeying for the same top spot. No wonder they were fighting! When we took your advice and stepped away from the fight, things got a lot better.

The first time, we got a lot of the "But Mom, he . . ." and "But Dad, she . . ." statements, but we'd learned from you that they were just playing us against each other. So my wife and I went and sat out on the deck for a while. They followed us, as you said they would, and tried to continue the fight. My wife and I eyed each other, took the car keys, and went for a drive, complete with a leisurely stop for coffee. When we got back, Laura was helping Samuel with his homework, and they were eating popcorn. Your advice works.

Matt, Pennsylvania

——————————— **Power Points** ———————————

- Rewire your typical morning conversations.
- Master your child's trigger points and your own.
- Disengage from the battle.
- Power down so your kid doesn't have to power up.

16

Redirecting the Power Surge

*How to encourage positive goals and
show your kids that they can use their
drive for power for a good purpose.*

They wrote him off as a dummy, a dawdler, a daydreamer. His teacher was always on his case.

"Albert, you need to pay attention. . . . Albert . . . Albert! If you don't pay attention, I'm going to call your mother."

Five minutes later: "Albert, bring your paper up to my desk right now. You seem to be doodling."

Upon receipt of the paper: "Can you explain this big E on your paper? And what's this little m and c doing there, and the two? That's it! I'm calling your parents today. You're absolutely not paying attention."

But nothing was further from the truth for the brilliant Albert Einstein, who used his power and determination to carve through the naysayers and bring us one of our most important scientific discoveries.

Then there's the lanky, geeky guy who lost 16 elections before he was ever elected president of the United States. But he powered on, because he wanted to use his power and determination to make a difference in his country and to serve those around him. If you look in your pocket and pull out a penny, you'll have physical evidence that Abraham Lincoln did well in life.

And then there's the kid who sat at the back of a room at the University of Buffalo, taking SAT exams and smoking half a pack of Salem cigarettes, thinking, *It's so cool these university guys let you smoke in the classroom.* This same guy couldn't even get into the university's night school—crafted for those who couldn't get into a regular university because of poor performance. That guy's name was Kevin Leman.

And behind each of those developing kids were parents who made a difference. Parents who believed in that child's unique talents and abilities and that their child's power-driven behavior could be transformed into a positive determination that could influence the world for the good.

It's How You Play Off Those Sparks

Nothing worthwhile in life is easy, and redirecting your powerful child won't be either. As an attention-getting and power-driven kid myself at one time, I'd be the first to tell you that. But the plan is simple, and this book has given you the road map for it.

However, what happens next is up to you. It's so easy to drift to what's comfortable, to what you did before. But when you do so with a powerful child, you've taken a couple of steps backward.

It's a little like the river that's valiantly trying to forge its way in a new channel and meets a lot of resistance, including the hard stone walls that rise on either side of it.

But if you redirect your child's power surges into positive urges, you *will* make daily progress. And by the time that child gets ready for college, finds a job, or launches off on a career track, you'll be saying, "Wow, it worked . . . and it was worth it."

How you play off the sparks your powerful child sends your way makes all the difference. When I came home at age 19 and announced that I was engaged to a young woman I hardly knew (not my beloved Sande), I didn't have two nickels to rub together and was far from being responsible enough to be married. But my mother didn't even lift an eyebrow. She just calmly asked for the green beans to be passed her way at dinner. Was she panicked inside? Probably. Did she show it? No. Or maybe it was just that I'd thrown her so many curveballs, I'd completely worn her down so nothing I said or did made her flinch.

Redirecting your power-driven child may seem like a daunting task. After all, that kid has led to many sleepless nights where you stared at the ceiling and asked, "Why, God? Why me? What went wrong here?"

But imagine what your kid with all that power and determination can do in the world someday if you hang in there and do the following:

- Address the underlying beliefs and life themes behind the child's behaviors.
- Encourage your child to use his natural abilities.
- Instead of punishing, focus on solutions that teach responsibility.
- Show you value your child's contribution in the family.

- Transform that power drive into determination that helps her stand up for what's right in her peer group.

That's a kid who might become an Albert Einstein or an Abraham Lincoln.

What Attention-Getting Kids Need: Involvement

Everyone wants to belong to a group, and your child is longing to belong to your family—as much as it may seem to the contrary. Belonging is a two-way street. It means you not only encourage your child, telling her you love her, but you also have positive expectations for her. As a part of your family, she wears your name and, as such, represents your family. That means as part of a group, she must fulfill certain basics.

All children need affirmation and involvement to grow. But you've picked up this book because you have a powerful child who's giving you a run for her money and you wonder what direction you both are going. Somewhere along the line, you've missed some opportunities to redirect her.

Now's the time to change that.

What Power-Driven Kids Need: Independence

Everyone wants to feel significant. We all want to contribute in meaningful ways. Although children of all ages seem to focus on taking from their parents, they also have a longing to give in their relationships too. If you find ways for them to give to you, your family, and others, they'll change their own beliefs about themselves.

That's because everyone wants to count.

Redirecting That Power-Surge Child

If you own the fact that your children are different and can't be treated equally, you're already on your way to redirecting your power-surge child.

For example, you'll give your firstborn privileges that the secondborn doesn't get. And you'll give the secondborn privileges and status that the thirdborn doesn't get. Does this mean that your kids aren't equal? No, but they play different roles in the family, just as you play a different role as the parent. Treating your children differently conveys to a child, "Mom and Dad don't treat us the same because we're different. I get it." If parents bend over backward to treat all kids the same, none of the kids will feel special or appreciated. And they'll grow up viewing reward as their right and themselves as socially equal to their parents.

They'll also resent the living heck out of a parent treating an older sibling differently. "How come he got to stay up late and go to that movie, and I didn't?"

Sound like a familiar conversation in your house? The kid who's mouthing off obviously feels dissed.

If you try to quell those words with a heavy hand by saying things like, "Because I said so," you'll up the power ante.

In the Leman family, I always answered with a little humor first: "Oh, honey, didn't you get the memo I sent last week? About how we love her so much more than we love you?"

The smart parent lays out the facts: "He's 16 and you're 14. I know you don't think there's a big difference in those two years, but there is. When you're 16, chances are we'll allow you to do things that he's doing. Patience is a great virtue." You smile. "I know you're impatient, and you know what? Your father was impatient with a capital *I*, and patience wasn't one of my strong suits either. But I'm getting better at it since I had you and your brother. You're teaching me a lot. Just know that for now, you can handle it, life is going to go on, and there will be better days ahead."

Whatever you do, don't be the wavering parent who makes a decision but then acquiesces when the kids start whining or complaining. Powerful kids can spot waffling adults a mile away. If you want to frustrate a powerful kid, give him the hope that there's a slim chance things might change. Then he'll work overtime to make it happen.

Instead, make a decision and don't back down.

If your child continues to argue with you (remember, fighting is an act that requires two people to cooperate), then he's a very powerful child. That means you have to stick to your guns even more.

"I have to hand it to you, Son, you're determined. You remind me of myself when I was your age. You put together a strong argument of why you should be able to do that."

> **Powerful kids can spot waffling adults a mile away.**

What are you doing? You're throwing the kid a bone for trying, but then you redirect his powerful behavior.

"It was a great try. It might have worked in someone else's home if they don't hold the same values as we do. But in our home, that doesn't get to second base. If I could hand out As in accordance with your strong-willed nature and how you attack the problem—the problem being your dad and me, of course—I'd have to admit I'd give you an A+. Sometime you're going to realize that these strengths you show off, including your ability to build a great case, could pay off if you point them in the right direction."

Just think, if you could turn his attention-getting into determination that helped him stand strong in his peer group, wouldn't you want that? The kind of child who could say, "No thanks" and stick to it when offered a snort of cocaine? Who would stay as mentally tough with his peers as he's being with you right now? Who doesn't need his peer group to be cool but is aiming straight as an arrow down his own chosen path?

Every child is striving for attention and to figure out their role in the family. Siblings love getting a leg up on each other. So the more you can emphasize the uniqueness of each child, the better. Give your older child a bedtime of even 15 to 20 minutes later than your secondborn, knowing that having some perks is critical for a firstborn, who carries a lot of responsibility. Give your secondborn an extra hour a week to play a computer game with a friend, since you know that friends are extremely important to middleborns. Take your baby of the family to the Cheese-breath Rodent's place and let him enjoy that "fine" pizza and a handful of tokens to go with it. He'll be one happy dude.

Your goal as a parent is to turn your attention-seeking child into a child who naturally garners attention because he's his own person. He doesn't waver based on his peer group, and he uses his attention-seeking behavior to make others feel welcomed and appreciated. Perhaps that attention-seeking kid will be the one who someday becomes a journalist who uncovers—and seeks to right—a societal ill.

What you can do

- Stick to the plan.
- Privately celebrate the victories that show you're making progress.
- Take one step at a time. Don't try to scale the whole mountain.
- Don't expect instant anything.

- Realize there will be days where you take two steps back in order to take three steps forward.

Especially for Parents of Teens (but It Applies to the Younger Kids Too)

Why do teens behave the way they do? Because, as stated earlier, all behavior serves a purpose. TreeHouse (http://www.treehouse youth.org) has done a fabulous job of identifying the goals of teen misbehavior, providing examples and steps you can take to encourage positive goals and beliefs in your teens. But it's also a great model to use with children of all ages, because it will help you learn to ask yourself very important questions:

- When my child acts in a certain way that drives me nuts, what do I usually do?
- How does my child usually respond to my action?
- What goal does the misbehavior accomplish for my child?
- What's the flip side of that goal? (In other words, what can we work toward together that will provide a more positive environment not only for my child and me but for everyone in the family?)[4]

Other books that parents of teenagers may find particularly helpful are *Running the Rapids* and *Have a New Teenager by Friday*, by yours truly.

Your Dreams—Or Your Child's?

Have you ever said to your child, "You can be anything you want to be and do anything you want to do in life"?

That sounds good, but it also conveys that we get to choose what we want to do in life. We all have limits—that's a part of being human. Some of us are physically limited; others are mentally, emotionally, or socially limited. That's why expectations need to be realistic.

And don't deny that you have expectations for your kids. We all do. Many of us project unfulfilled dreams onto our kids because of negative things that have happened to us in life or things we felt we missed out on. In the movie *A Cinderella Story*, both main characters are trapped by expectations. Sam (played by Hilary Duff) is trapped into being a servant for her stepmom, because she wants to fulfill her dream of going to Princeton. Austin is trapped by his father's expectations that he'll get a football scholarship and then, after college, return to help his father run his business. The breaking point in the movie is when Austin leaves the football field.

His father says, "You're throwing away your dream."

"No, Dad," Austin says, looking his father directly in the eye, "I'm throwing away yours."

Are you trying to live your dream

> **Your child deserves her own life instead of trying to fulfill your wishes.**

through your child? If so, realize that every person is different. Your child deserves her own life instead of trying to fulfill your wishes.

That's why it's so important for parents to realize that each child has her own individual bent—a propensity to do well in certain things and not as well (if anything at all) in other things.

I tell college students that the key to success in life is finding that one thing they do extremely well and then working to get better at it. But it has to be *their dream*, not yours.

Expectations that stay high and are unrealistic will, over a period of time, defeat your child. Then she'll actively try to gain negative attention (attention-getting behavior), get in your face, or just ignore you (power-driven behavior). Or she'll move to the stage of revenge ("I'll get back at you for that") and then on to the "whatever" stage ("It doesn't matter what I say or think, you'll do what you want, so who gives a rip about life anyway?").

When a child is very young, he doesn't really know what things he's interested in. That's the time to explore lots of different options—but only one at a time. However, note his natural talents first. For example, you probably wouldn't want your boy who spends hours doodling with crayons to sign up for baseball. You might want to involve him in a community art class for children.

As your child grows older and enters school, allow her interests to develop in her mind. Instead of pushing your child to join an activity, say, "Wow, there are a lot of options of things to get involved in, now that you're in school. Are there any you're particularly interested in? If so, which ones?"

By this response, you're conveying two things to your child:

1. The choice is hers of whether to get involved at all. Note that by saying what you did, you're not pushing her into excessive activities. Some children especially need a lot of quiet and reflective time; others are social critters from the beginning. My rule, for the sake of everyone in the family, has been one activity per child per semester.

2. If she does decide to get involved, she can choose an activity that is of interest to her, rather than you slanting her interest toward one you think she should do.

If your child does choose an activity, then the responsibility, the goal-setting, and the expectations ought to come from the child herself—not from you. But you, smart parent, are going to set the limits on how many interests can be pursued at once.

What you can do

- Encourage your child to explore activities that are of interest to her.

Her patterns of interest ought to dictate what activity she gets involved in. Don't make her take ballet just because you did. Maybe she likes skateboarding better, and the idea of a pink tutu simply gets a raised eyebrow. If so, there's your clue. A quiet statement such as "I saw that you seemed to really enjoy trying out those band instruments" can help your child in fine-tuning her interests.

- In casual conversation, mention areas in which she shines.

"I saw your eyes light up at the idea of speech meets. Ever since you were young, you always loved giving speeches. You'd even write up speeches for your stuffed animals and then deliver them in different voices to represent the animals. Giving speeches seems very natural for you."

- Let the child's interests do the leading, not yours.

It's almost an art form to be able to encourage kids to continue to grow in an area where they obviously have talent. Statements such as "My, you've been swimming so great this year that I know you'll be going to state next year. I'm so proud to be your mom!" put unjust pressure on your child. And since your child is a powerful kid, the first thing she'll do is narrow her eyes and think, *Oh yeah? I'm not going to be in swimming at all next year, then.*

That kind of statement also says, "I hold you in high esteem because you've achieved something."

But is that really what you want to convey to your child? That you will only love, appreciate, and accept her when she achieves?

Statements such as "Wow, it looks like you're really enjoying swimming this year. I marvel at the talents God has given you" are warm and affirming, focus on the child's joy in the event, and give credit where credit is due. And your child smiles, encouraged by your support of her.

So the next time your 8-year-old daughter goes exploring in the woods and brings back a deer skull, what will you say?

"Ew, that's so gross. It's probably crawling with vermin. Go take that outside right now!" Or "Well, would you look at that? Where did you find that? . . . I'd never have guessed there would be deer back there. I wonder how old the skull is. If you want to clean it up so we can take a better look, you could use the sink in the garage. Oh, and here's a toothbrush and some antibacterial soap."

All it takes is counting to 10 before you open your mouth and a consideration of what matters most in the long run—your relationship with your child.

The Star of the Show

Let's say you have four children. Each of them has one activity per semester. That adds up to a lot of running around in your SUV. So you need to have realistic expectations not only of your kids but also of yourself as a parent. What price will you pay for your child to play weekend soccer? To be on a city team or a traveling team? To be in swim meets? To take riding lessons? To compete in dance?

If one of your kids plays soccer and the others don't, you can't leave your other kids—ages 3, 8, and 9—home alone, can you? How much of yourself and your family time are you willing to give to that one activity?

Now, there are exceptions—kids in the seventh and eighth grades, for example, who have major college potential in a sport or in music. Those kids go to basketball camps, may have special one-on-one tutoring, and may even go to a special prep school away from home in order to take advantage of great teaching and competition at that higher level. If that's something your child wants and she is willing to work that hard, then all power to that powerful child. You should do all you can—without making the rest of the family sacrifice—to support her. However, it has to be *her dream*, not yours.

But the average kid won't end up in the NBA, making millions, wearing $5,000 suits and $1,000 ties. And trying to make one kid in the family the star of the show only creates resentment and rivalries for the others in the family. If all the attention is focused on one, the others can't help but think, *Hey, I got the short end of the stick here.* Then the natural attention-getting behavior turns into ramped-up attention-getting. If the cry for attention is ignored, that child will become a powerful child.

> **Powerful children are ones who not only gain attention but make you pay attention.**

Powerful children are ones who not only gain attention but make you pay attention. They can become the stars of your family show. Don't let their antics overshadow the other children in your home.

Instead, acknowledge the individual, unique bents of each child, and support each one in their talents.

Transforming Power Surges to Positive Urges

Moving a kid from power surges to positive urges isn't easy, but it's simple.

Your kid cops an attitude. You don't fight back. You don't argue.

But then, four hours later, when he demands to be taken somewhere, what do you say? "I don't feel like taking you anywhere today." You respond straightforwardly but in a low-key manner.

When you stay with the program, your child starts to see this as a day he doesn't get what he wants. Sooner or later, a light has to go on in the kid's head. He starts to think, *This isn't paying off, is it?* Especially since you now know that his attention-getting and powerful behavior is designed to make you cave in and do what he wants.

It won't be long before he chooses another path. That path may be to try to up the ante and become more powerful and stubborn. If so, even more reason for you to stick to the plan and not give in. Over time he'll see that if he chooses a different path—cooperation with you—he'll be better off.

Many of these powerful kids have never been told that they have skills—that they could accomplish something great in life if they tried. They've certainly got the power and determination to go far.

I got terrible grades in school, so I equated my skills with my grades. I didn't think I had any. It wasn't until that teacher told me I could use my skills for a positive purpose that I even thought, *Skills? I've got skills?* That's because powerful children are insecure children. Their life theme is, *I only count when I'm on top, when I'm in the spotlight.*

Solidly in Your Kid's Court

You of all people have to be solidly entrenched in your kid's court. I can't tell you how many children and teenagers I've talked with over the years who have said, "I could never talk to my mom/dad about this, because they wouldn't understand." It's important to get inside your kid's head—to help figure out the life theme that informs what he does. Your child needs a real-life coach, and the best one of all is you. You're the one who knows your child's individual bent, his talents and abilities. Even in a few minutes a day, you can encourage his positive goals and healthy beliefs about himself.

Only a very mature child would think to write down her goals in life. So why not keep a little notebook to benefit your child? Record the following:

- emerging talents
- milestone events
- times you catch her doing good
- unique ways she contributes to your family
- other encouraging details

Then give the notebook to your child as a surprise on her birthday or any other special occasion. Bet you anything she'll want you to start another one for the next year. Because most of all, your powerful child needs to know that you think she's special, that she's an important part of your family, that you believe in her and her talents, and that you're convinced she's put on this earth for a purpose—to make a contribution to the world that only she can make.

A Good Heart

A mom I've known for years told me a heartwarming story about her daughter, Katy.

> When I picked up my normally quiet daughter from school today, she was all smiles. I hadn't even pulled away from the curb before she blurted out, "Mom, I just had the best day of all!"
>
> "Really? Tell me more about that," I said.
>
> "My teacher, Miss Karen, pulled me aside. She told me I reminded her a lot of herself when she was my age. She said that what the popular girls did and said didn't seem to matter to me. That I treated everybody equally, and other kids respected me because of it. She said I was always myself and I stayed steady. And that impressed her."
>
> As a mom, of course, I swelled with pride. What mom wouldn't, just a little?
>
> But the tears of joy came when my daughter continued. "That means a lot, Mom, because Miss Karen is like me."

You see, Katy is Asian, and her teacher is African American. They are two of the few non-Caucasians in their school. Katy was picked on in younger grades because she was "different." But she also had two loving parents who taught her how to stand up for herself, how to see the attention of others in a positive light, how to gain attention in a positive way, and at what stage to get teachers involved. By third grade, she'd gained the respect of all the classroom bullies, who no longer bullied her. One, in fact, said with awe, "You're the toughest girl I know." And Katy is indeed determined. She's a powerful child who won't back down . . . but she does it quietly and respectfully.

That's why the teacher's comment meant so much to Katy. She

could have responded to the bullies by fighting back; instead she merely eyed them, turned her back, and walked away. As a result, she has emerged as a natural leader in her class, with the respect of all.

Katy's teacher, Miss Karen, has a tradition of asking her students to come up with adjectives to describe each child on their birthday. The adjectives that came up most frequently for Katy were a good heart, trustworthy, a leader, and friends with everybody.

And Katy lives out those words with relentless determination.

The day after Miss Karen pulled Katy aside, the popular girls in her class were gossiping about another girl, who was new to the school. Katy walked up to the new girl and said, "Hi, I'm Katy. I'm sitting over there. Would you like to sit with me?"

It was a small gesture but a world-changing one for that new girl. All because of a girl with "a good heart."

When each of the five Leman kids stood up for kids who got picked on, I felt the same way as that mom. So when you catch your child being kind to others, make sure you reaffirm that kindness: "I'm so blessed to have a daughter like you who cares enough to stick up for others. Your teacher told me what happened today. That shows me how strong of a person you are. I'm so proud of you."

Your child might look a little embarrassed, but inside she's thinking, *Wow, I just did what came into my head. And Mom gets it. It's so cool my teacher noticed and said something. You know, there's another girl who seems kinda down. Maybe I could ask her to sit at my lunch table tomorrow. . . .*

You see how smart your child is?

Keep your child's spark igniting in a positive direction, and she'll use her power to benefit others.

That's about as close of a guarantee as you can get in life.

Powerful Ideas That Work

David's my second child and the baby of the family. He's always been a handful. I could never have any conversation without him interrupting.

When he turned 8, things got really bad. Once, when I was talking with my dad, David stepped between us and said, "Grandpa, I'm going to burn your barn down." My dad was shocked, and my jaw dropped. Our conversation stopped. Neither of us knew what to say, but the kid had our attention.

A month later, my mom invited me to one of your seminars. That's when I realized I'd allowed David to go from attention-seeking to powerful. He's the classic secondborn you talk about. His older brother outshines him in just about everything, so he decided he had to go the exact opposite way.

A couple days after I got home, I talked with David and said, "I could be wrong, but I think these are the reasons you're doing what you're doing," and I laid out what I'd learned. When David admitted he never felt good enough, I had my answer. My husband and I are now brainstorming how we can encourage David in a positive direction instead of encouraging all his negative attention-getting. We know it won't be easy, but for the first time since he was a toddler, we have a workable plan.

Teresa, Arizona

Power Points

- Everyone wants to belong.
- Everyone wants to count.
- Everyone has natural abilities and can make a contribution.
- Everyone can be encouraged toward the good—with the proper motivation.

Conclusion

You Can Do It!

*Don't forget the fun. The family that
plays together stays together.*

Some families don't have fun. We Lemans try to have fun every-where. When we go into a restaurant, it's not unusual for us to cheer—clap, hoot, and holler—for our waiter or waitress when he or she arrives at our table. We get to know them quickly—find out their name, what they did when they weren't waiting tables, and what they'd love to be doing five years from now.

That's because all of us know that we have a choice in life—we can choose to be all about ourselves, or we can choose to engage others and try to make a difference in their lives.

If you break the communication barrier, you find out that people are people. No matter our age, we all want to belong, to be wanted, to be needed, and to be appreciated. And we all need to lighten up sometimes and have fun.

Want a Fun Family Dinner?

If you want to have some great family fun and also get inside your kids' heads and hearts—without them suspecting you're doing so—you can use a trick from ol' Adler himself (see, I told you knowing something about him would be practical).

Adler believed that if someone walked through his door, and he knew their birth order and asked about their early childhood memories, he could predict how that person viewed life.

If you ask the three siblings in your home to talk about the same event, they'd all report it differently. All of us tend to see life through our own glasses, and they're different prescriptions, based on our life themes.

So try this at your next family dinner. Say, "You know, kids, I was thinking about an early memory of mine," and share it. Then say, "Hey, what's the earliest memory you have, Josh? What about you, Amanda? And you, Nick?"

> **If you ask the three siblings in your home to talk about the same event, they'd all report it differently.**

With your firstborn, I can guarantee one of those early memories will be a negative one—such as falling off a bike or ladder and breaking his arm. Other typical memories of firstborns are ones of achievement—recognition, a star on a paper, figuring a puzzle out. These point out that even at an early age, firstborns are susceptible to thinking first about the negatives—they take life more seriously than the other birth orders. They also have a driving need to achieve.

Why can't firstborns just think about positive things? Because the nature of the firstborn is that he spends a long part of his life being the standard bearer, corrected by both his mom and his dad.

He's been told, "I don't care what they did. You're the oldest. I expect more of you." Or "Don't give me that. You're 13. Your brother is 9. I would think you'd be more responsible." Firstborns are only tapping into the higher standards they've been held to as they recount their memories.

As for middleborns, their memories usually involve their friends and are typically less about family members. That's because at home, the middleborn is often the invisible one, with the firstborn and the baby both being stars of the family show for different reasons. A common memory is of negotiating something, or of having to wear her older sister's prom dress because it still looked new and her folks didn't want to spend another $400 on a dress.

Other memories for middleborns would be ones of rebellion or where they were revealed as unique individuals. They're the ones most likely to remember Mom announcing, "Here's Steve, my firstborn, and my baby, Jennifer. And then there's Jane." The middleborn is truly stuck in the middle, and that's why parents would be wise to give middleborns additional time with them, away from the other siblings.

Babies of the family will remember birthdays, surprises, presents, Christmases, special days, and events. That's because those are consistent with a baby's life view. Babies have never met a stranger; they're all about where the next party is. They didn't have their parents hovering over them (Mom and Dad were too tired by baby number three to hover), and besides, two other siblings were a buffer between them and Mom and Dad. The baby often got off scot-free in family skirmishes: "He's a baby. He doesn't know any better."

Firstborns have adults (their parents) as their model from the get-go. In families of two or more children, each birth order is more influenced by the sibling(s) above them.

All Good (and Bad) Things Will Come to An End

As parents, we can get so caught up in the everyday struggles for attention, power, and control that we wonder, *Will this ever end?*

I guarantee you this stage of in-the-trenches parenting will be over faster than you can imagine. Your powerful child will grow up. And everything that you've taught her will become part of what she carries with her into adulthood.

When things get stressful in your home, you can always break the ice by having fun. Just as an apple a day keeps the doctor away, a dose of fun keeps the family together. Remember, your kids are kids. They need fun every single day.

So do you.

So many of us, though, act like a prison warden carrying a big stick: "You better hop to it, or else." But you, parent, should see yourself in the role of relationship maker. Part of forming a relationship is providing fun. Even my wife, Sande, who is much more serious than I am, is good at telling me, "Leemie, you've got to lighten up. It's not a big deal." And she's always right when she says it. (She is a firstborn, after all.)

Everybody in your family nest has a purpose for being there. Some of your kids will slide through your home like sorbet going down your throat, smooth as she goes. Others are more like peanut buster parfaits—full of bumpy, nutty surprises.

My cousin once reminded me of a wedding we attended as youngsters. As we stood outside the church, everybody else threw rice. I threw gravel.

But people do change, and powerful kids can be shaped to become powerful influencers who help others. When I received an award in my adult years from my high school for being a difference

256

maker, some of the relatives who had been guests at that wedding showed up. They had to see it to believe it, since they knew my checkered history at the school.

Take a look around. Everyone has someone in their family who, like me, was written off by others early in life because he was such a handful. Now he's the town baker, a respectable city official, or the town attorney.

Change is not only possible but highly probable for powerful kids. All it takes is someone like you to believe in them and to help transform their attention-seeking, power-driven behavior into a determination that doesn't give up until a task is accomplished.

Then they'll go far.

Just watch them.

Top 10 Power Points

1. Every family has a powerful child.

2. Power comes in different packages.

3. Genes, environment, and birth order are powerful influencers.

4. Every child develops his or her own screenplay on life.

5. All children seek attention—positively or negatively.

6. Kids only misbehave if doing so works.

7. Win their cooperation.

8. Rewire your parenting strategies.

9. Transform negative power surges into positive urges.

10. They don't care what you know . . . until they know that you care.

Notes

1. Margery Williams, *The Velveteen Rabbit* (New York: Doubleday, 1922), 5.

2. See Matthew 6:15.

3. Larry Nisan, "The Four Mistaken Goals of Children's Misbehaviour—Diagnosis and Remediation," PsychotherapyInstitute.com, http://ultimatelifecoach.net/pdf/TheFourMistakenGoalsofChildren.pdf, accessed January 28, 2013.

4. See TreeHouse, "Why Teens Misbehave," 2012, http://www.treehouseyouth.org/page.aspx?pid=513.

About
Dr. Kevin Leman

An internationally known psychologist, radio and television personality, and speaker, **Dr. Kevin Leman** has taught and entertained audiences worldwide with his wit and commonsense psychology.

The *New York Times* bestselling and award-winning author of *Have a New Kid by Friday*, *Have a New Husband by Friday*, *Have a New You by Friday*, *Sheet Music*, and *The Birth Order Book* has made thousands of house calls through radio and television programs, including *Fox & Friends*, *The View*, Bill Bennett's *Morning in America*, Fox's *The Morning Show*, *Today*, *The 700 Club*, *Oprah*, CBS's *The Early Show*, CNN's *American Morning*, *Life Today* with James Robison, and *Focus on the Family*. Dr. Leman has also served as a contributing family psychologist to *Good Morning America*.

Dr. Leman is the founder and president of Couples of Promise, an organization designed and committed to help couples remain happily married. His professional affiliations include the American Psychological Association, the American Federation of Television and Radio Artists, and the North American Society of Adlerian Psychology.

In 2003, the University of Arizona awarded Dr. Leman the highest award they can give to one of their own: the Distinguished Alumnus Award. In 2010, North Park University awarded him an honorary Doctor of Humane Letters degree.

Dr. Leman received his bachelor's degree in psychology from the University of Arizona, where he later earned his master's and doctorate degrees. Originally from Williamsville, New York, he and his wife, Sande, live in Tucson, Arizona. They have five children and two grandchildren.

For information regarding speaking availability, business consultations, seminars, or the annual Learn, Laugh, and Love cruise, please contact:

Dr. Kevin Leman
P.O. Box 35370
Tucson, Arizona 85740
Phone: (520) 797-3830
Fax: (520) 797-3809
www.birthorderguy.com
www.drleman.com

Resources by
Dr. Kevin Leman

Books for Adults

Have a New Kid by Friday
Have a New Husband by Friday
Have a New Teenager by Friday
Have a New You by Friday
The Birth Order Book
The Way of the Wise
What a Difference a Mom Makes
What a Difference a Daddy Makes
Parenting Your Powerful Child
Under the Sheets
Sheet Music
Making Children Mind without Losing Yours
It's a Kid, Not a Gerbil!
Born to Win
Sex Begins in the Kitchen
7 Things He'll Never Tell You . . . But You Need to Know
What Your Childhood Memories Say about You
Running the Rapids

The Way of the Shepherd (written with William Pentak)

Becoming the Parent God Wants You to Be

Becoming a Couple of Promise

A Chicken's Guide to Talking Turkey with Your Kids about Sex (written with Kathy Flores Bell)

First-Time Mom

Step-parenting 101

Living in a Stepfamily without Getting Stepped On

The Perfect Match

Be Your Own Shrink

Stopping Stress before It Stops You

Single Parenting That Works

Why Your Best Is Good Enough

Smart Women Know When to Say No

Books for Children, with Kevin Leman II

My Firstborn, There's No One Like You

My Middle Child, There's No One Like You

My Youngest, There's No One Like You

My Only Child, There's No One Like You

My Adopted Child, There's No One Like You

My Grandchild, There's No One Like You

DVD/Video Series for Group Use

Have a New Kid by Friday

Making Children Mind without Losing Yours (Christian—parenting edition)

Making Children Mind without Losing Yours (Mainstream—public school teacher edition)

Value-Packed Parenting

Making the Most of Marriage
Running the Rapids
Single Parenting That Works
Bringing Peace and Harmony to the Blended Family

DVDs for Home Use

Straight Talk on Parenting
Why You Are the Way You Are
Have a New Husband by Friday
Have a New You by Friday

Available at 1-800-770-3830

or

www.drleman.com

or

www.birthorderguy.com.

Visit DrLeman.com

for more information, resources, and videos from his popular books.

Follow Dr. Kevin Leman on

 Dr Kevin Leman

 drleman

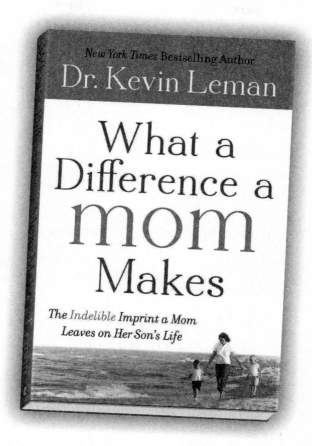